In Delilah's Eyes:
Dog Training
from
A Dog's Perspective

A Training Manual for Humans

Cheryl Falkenburry

Center Hill School Press

For Dogs, Cats

and Their Humans

Don't get rid of the animal,
Get rid of the problem behavior.

In Delilah's Eyes: Dog Training from a Dog's Perspective
A training manual for humans
by Cheryl Falkenburry

www.indelilahseyes.com

Published in the US by:

Center Hill School Press
Palmyra, VA 22963

www.centerhillschool.com

ISBN 978-0-615-28259-6 paperback

Printed by Signature Book Printing, www.sbpbooks.com

Dedication

To Sunshine, the shelter dog who came into my life in 1979 and started me on my path to dog training; to my husband and children who assisted with rehabilitating numerous foster dogs over the years; to my friends who encouraged and supported me through the task of writing this book; and to Delilah, a hand-me-down dog who has been a constant, loving, patient, and devoted canine companion.

Contents

Introduction

Wouldn't it be nice to get into our dogs' heads—to see the world through their eyes? Imagine the knowledge we would gain. What if I told you with just a little education and no psychic ability, you *can* understand some of what your dog is thinking?

Working with dogs most of my life has provided many opportunities to learn more about their world. By observing, training, and living with dogs, I believe they taught me more than I taught them. I spent years trying to look at the world through their eyes, which led me to write this book from a dog's perspective. After all, I owe most of my education to the dogs, and as far as I'm concerned, "Going to the dogs," is a good thing!

Delilah, a St. Bernard, has been my greatest doggie teacher. She came to me after living in a variety of households. Obviously she wasn't perfect, having been passed from home-to-home so many times, but I'm not perfect either. We were, however, perfect for each other as we worked together teaching people and animals. She was a great leader among dogs in her younger years, and watching her in action taught me a great deal about domesticated dogs and how they communicate.

Delilah is now retired and spends her days resting at my feet while I write. She is the inspiration behind this book, and it is written in her voice. My goal is not to anthropomorphize (humanize animals) by writing this book as if a dog could think through many of the ideas presented. Dogs tend to live in the here and now and don't give a lot of thought to their actions. However, I felt a book which took a light-hearted look at the world from a dog's standpoint might be of value to people since so often, right or wrong, we do put human qualities on our dogs. This book does not contain a lot of learning theory, just some basic training steps and a little glimpse of the world, at least *In Delilah's Eyes.*

Cheryl

Delilah Speaks

I know that humans believe dog behavior can be mind-boggling, but really, you humans are often totally baffling to dogs. One day a dog jumps up on you to say hello, and you hug and greet him with a smile. The next day the dog greets you with a jump and is met with screams and punishment over a $500 designer something-or-other. Come on people—make up your minds!

Dogs look at life from a different perspective than humans, and that's where the trouble begins. Most dogs are willing to learn the rules of the human world, but people have to show us what they are and the benefits to following them. Otherwise, we will just do what dogs do. It's not misbehaving in our minds; it's just responding to the environment around us and satisfying our needs. If a dog eats a shoe while you are gone, it doesn't mean he's angry; it means he missed you and this shoe reminded him of you, or simply...he was bored. If a dog pees on your bed after you pack your bags for a trip, it doesn't mean she's getting even; it means that she's nervous about all the activity. Your bed smells like you, and it is comforting. Peeing relieves some of the nervous tension. There's no revenge involved (that's a human quality I'll never understand), only an attempt to calm down in an uncomfortable situation.

This book is a simple look at how dogs view the world and guidelines to help change both human (yes, humans need to change their behavior too) and animal behavior in order to enhance the relationship between dogs and people.

Since Cheryl understands how you humans think better than me, she added her comments where she felt necessary in the "Paws to Ponder" boxes. We didn't worry whether using "he" or "she" was appropriate and mixed things up to include both. Please remember as you read this book that I don't have a strong command of the English language, so if you don't agree with what I've written, call Cheryl, not me. She must have gotten something wrong in the translation.

Delilah

Chapter 1

The Differing Worlds of Dogs and Humans

The Differing Worlds of Dogs and Humans

T*he monster approached with staring, dark eyes. Upon its head was a strange lumpy growth. In its hand was a long lethal weapon. Smoke billowed from its mouth. As it crept nearer, its hairy lips parted in a sneer. My body stiffened, and I took a few steps backward. Clearly, this was someone or something not to be trusted. Its hand plunged out in a fist, just inches away from my face. I looked back and forth between this dangerous creature and my partner, weighing my options—fight or flight?*

What would you do if you were in this situation? What if someone near and dear to you was standing right there with you? Could you run and leave her to fend off this horrifying beast alone or would you stand and fight?

This scene isn't something out of a horror movie. It's something that happened to me. My name is Delilah, and I'm a St. Bernard. I'm here to help humans see the world from a dog's perspective in order to enhance the human-dog bond. Lack of understanding is the root of many problems between dogs and their humans. Dogs don't see the world the same way people do—after all, we are dogs. Let me put what happened to me in the above situation in human terms.

The monster is a person whom I did not know. The person made direct eye contact with me as he approached, which is a threat in the dog world. The growth on his head was an odd looking hat—a cowboy hat which I had never encountered before. The lethal weapon was simply an umbrella, which can be a very threatening object when one is not familiar with its purpose. The man was smoking a pipe, an odd habit indeed to a dog. The lips parted signifies a friendly greeting in the human world—it's a smile. In the dog world, however, a bearing of the teeth is a challenge. Many dogs learn to associate a smile on their human's face with positive outcomes, but dogs who have not been exposed to a lot of people can only resort to their dog instincts and experiences. In this case, the person had a beard, which partially covered facial features making the intent of the person unclear even to the most human-savvy dog. A hand plunged forward to be sniffed is something humans are taught to do when greeting a dog. However, dogs feel threatened when an object is thrust into their face unless they have been taught that a hand coming towards them is a positive event. If a dog has been abused in the past, a fist may not be taken as an invitation to sniff.

What is a dog to do when put in this situation? A dog with a high pack sense will not want to run and leave his human (part of the pack) to face this threatening character alone; therefore, there is a good chance the dog will go into a protection stance and may bite if she deems it necessary. A dog who decides to run, may realize she cannot because the leash prevents the flight—leaving only one option in the dog's mind: fight.

Humans are often confused when their normally friendly dog suddenly lashes out, but most of the time there is a very logical reason for it in the dog's mind. Unfortunately, in the human world, biting is a big no-no, and the dog, who was only doing what dogs do, often suffers severe consequences.

What could have been done differently to improve the situation? The person in this scenario had good intentions. He approached with a smile, pleased to see his friend and her dog out for a walk. He wanted to say hello to the dog, and presented a hand to sniff. If humans understood how dogs view the world, I'm sure they would approach dogs in a different manner.

In this particular scenario, the human could have removed his hat as he saw me and my person walking towards him. To decrease my apprehension, he should have avoided eye conact, indicating to me that he meant no harm. Sometimes the best way to greet a dog is to act like the dog is not there at all. Standing still and allowing the dog to come up to your hand and sniff is a much better approach than reaching out to the dog. This allows the dog time to see that you understand her needs and will allow her to say hello if she so desires. If the man had moved the umbrella to the side away from me and held it close to his leg, it would have seemed less threatening.

Watching a dog's body language is important. I was giving all sorts of clues as the man approached. I stiffened my body and held my tail high—an alert stance. Some dogs might tuck their tail and put their ears back in a sign of fear. I took a few steps backward, and my eyes were darting back and forth between the man, my human, and potential avenues of flight. All these body signals, however slight, are an indication that a dog is uncomfortable with a situation. If the man had noticed them, he could have stopped, allowed me and my person to approach him as he gave all the clues mentioned earlier to show he was not a threat.

Of course, not all the responsibility is on the person coming to greet the dog. If my human had taken the time to train and socialize me so a hat, an umbrella, a hand to the nose, and a smile were familiar, I may have handled the situation better. Plus my human should have been paying attention to all the signals my body was giving her. Then she could have helped me accept the man's approach by asking me to sit, giving me treats, and showing me she was in control of the situation.

Humans get very caught up socially in their own greetings and often forget to watch what their dogs are telling them. If my human had been paying attention she could have redirected me to positive behavior so I could overcome my fear. I now know about all these things, but back then I was clueless and so was the person I lived with at the time.

Training a dog to live in a human world goes beyond teaching the dog to sit. Dogs need to have positive experiences around a variety of people and objects to become a confident, well-behaved canine citizen. Don't bring a dog into your house and expect she will know what to do. That's usually when life takes a turn for the worse for many dogs. Learning how to communicate with your dog in a way the dog understands will help you build a trusting and loving relationship with your canine companion. You're taking a great first step by reading this book, so keep reading, and then start teaching. You'll be amazed at what both you and your dog will learn.

Paws to Ponder

Dogs are going to continue doing what dogs do naturally until the people in their lives show them how to behave properly in the human world. Dogs don't have an instruction manual on how to behave around humans; it's up to the humans to teach dogs what is expected.

Dogs gain confidence by having positive experiences. Take time to show your dog what items in the world are all about. Open an umbrella and set it on the ground. If the dog is scared, start with it closed. Put some food near any item your dog is worried about. Help the dog learn that there is no need to fear the item. As a dog gains confidence, she will become more relaxed and a safe canine citizen in the community. (See the chapter on *Helping the Fearful Dog* to learn more about helping a dog get over fears.)

Chapter 2

Lead On: A World with No Jumping, Begging, or Demanding Dogs

Lead On: A World with No
Jumping, Begging, or Demanding Dogs

In my lifetime, I have had numerous humans in charge of my care. Each one decided for whatever reason that caring for me was too arduous a task and passed me on to the next interested party. Many people think that living with a St. Bernard is all fun and games, since we are such big, goofy, and lovable looking dogs. However, we can also be big, drooling trouble makers. I finally landed in the home of a dog trainer, Cheryl. Her job was to evaluate me and decide why I had been passed from family to family. She would then advise the rescue agency as to what type of family could potentially provide a forever home. Fortunately for me, Cheryl decided *her* home was just the home I needed. She was right. I needed someone who understood me—who accepted me for who I am, but who also was a strong leader. Cheryl showed me what was expected and taught me behaviors that were beneficial to me. I had to work for everything, but I didn't mind. I discovered the job paid well and had the added benefit of keeping both my mind and body busy, which kept me out of trouble.

Being a strong leader doesn't mean leading by force. Leaders take charge by showing strength in character—by showing team members understanding, patience, and kindness while guiding them through the rules of the establishment. Rules are needed in any society to help guide the members. Some feel giving dogs rules is cruel, but dogs want rules. *We need rules.* Rules help a dog understand what is expected. It gives us comfort to know where our place is in the pack (dog word for "team"). Dogs who come into a household without rules often feel they need to take charge because no one else seems to be in control. You do NOT want your dog to feel this way. Set rules the first day a dog comes into your home and make sure everyone in the house abides by them—both humans and dogs. Show the dog there are rewards to be earned when rules are followed—I personally like to be scratched behind my ear when I lie down at my human's feet. I learned this gets my human's attention instead of pushing at her hand with my nose or pawing at her, which only makes her turn away from me.

When I first came to her house, I pawed at her, I pushed her with my nose, all to have her cross her arms and turn away from me. Not one word, not a single glare, she just ignored me. I hate to be ignored! When I demanded attention before, all my other humans petted me, pushed me, glared at me, or said "no." All those responses gave me the attention I craved, so I continued the behavior. But this ignoring thing I didn't like. One day I finally gave up and sat wondering about this strange human, and what do you know, my new human said "Yes" in a quick soft voice and started scratching me behind my ear. I discovered she uses that word when I perform a behavior she likes. I finally figured out that sitting or lying down at her feet almost always got the attention I was seeking. Once I figured out the benefits to following the rules, I repeated more desirable behaviors to receive my reward.

I admit dogs are pretty selfish beings. We live for food. We know we need it to survive. If you show me that behaving a certain way will ensure that I will continue to receive my most vital resource—food—then I will continue to do that behavior. Some humans think using food in training is bribery, but I like to think of it as earning my salary. If I do certain tasks throughout the day, I know I will be given a salary—my food. It may come in small treats throughout the day or in a bowl twice a day. When I first came to my forever home, I had to work for every morsel of food. I didn't get any meals in a bowl. All throughout the day, my human would help me learn to do certain things— sit, down, stay and so much more. Every time I figured out what she wanted, she said "Yes" in a quick soft voice and gave me a handful of my food which was measured each morning into a container on the counter. You bet I wanted to figure things out so I could get my food. After a few weeks when I figured out the rules, I got less food throughout the day and received my meals in a bowl like the other dogs in the house. I felt like it was a promotion! I had trained and learned the ropes so I could be trusted and no longer had to work for every single bite of food. If any of the dogs in my house start to forget the rules, a hand-feeding regimen is started again. Of course, I'm so wonderful, I learned the rules quickly and stick to them...most of the time.

Dogs know that food is important for survival. They have other objects in their life that may hold the same high status which can also be used in training. Oreo, a Border Collie mix friend, lived for his ball. When his human threw the ball, he was in heaven. He would do any behavior to just have her throw that ball one more time. Make note of what your dog enjoys—food, toys, attention, play, etc., and use those rewards throughout training.

One key to getting a dog to follow your leadership is to demonstrate the benefit involved by using what your dog loves most. Control the benefit; control the dog. If I want my dinner, I have to sit. If I want to go for a walk, I have to sit at the door and wait. If I want to say hello to my human when she comes home, I have to be calm. The benefit may differ depending on the situation, but I know if I want to receive a certain reward, I have to behave a certain way. I know this because my human took the time to show me.

If I jumped and acted crazy at the door, she ignored me. Acted like I wasn't even there!—and trust me that's tough to do when one hundred pounds of St. Bernard is dancing around your feet. But my human is a good leader. She knew that if she ignored me when I was crazy and then paid attention to me when I was calm, I would repeat the calm behavior so I could get what I wanted, in this situation—her attention. Also by her turning her back and looking away, she was giving the classic dog body language for, "I want nothing to do with you right now." That kind of language I understand. I use it all the time with visiting dogs who are crazy. I turn my head away, until they leave me alone or at least calm down and play appropriately. Most dogs understand this kind of language much better than yelling and pushing.

When Merry, a cute little black poodle, first started visiting our house, she tried to launch herself into my human's lap. Merry was met with body blocks. My human turned her body, crossed her arms, and blocked Merry's attempt to jump on her lap. Little Merry would slide to the floor instead of landing in a cozy lap each time, but she was persistent and would try again and again. Each time, she was met with body blocks so no lap was available. Merry finally learned what I learned, sit at the human's feet and then you get the attention you desire. Because of Merry's energy, it took a lot more repetitions than it did to change my pawing and nosing behavior. The more body blocks she received, the harder she tried to jump. She figured it always worked before, so she just needed to do it with more intensity. When that didn't work, she sat down quite perplexed at the whole situation, and my human said that lovely quick soft "Yes" word. Merry was then invited on her lap. It took a lot more repetitions before Merry finally got it and realized if she just sat, she would be invited. I'd like to think that I'm smarter than Merry and that's why I caught on quicker, but I really think it had more to do with I'm somewhat lazy and just gave up sooner than she did!

A good dog-leader knows that too many loud words and lots of hand movements will excite dogs. Quiet leadership, using the body to block, is the best way to lead. If you push at your dog with your hands, your dog may misinterpret this as an invitation to play. Have you ever watched two dogs playing? Sometimes one dog will paw at the other dog to get them started. If you "paw" at your dog with your hands, you are giving them the opposite signal than you intended. Cross your arms, push your shoulder forward if you are sitting, put your nose up in the air, and look away. Your dog will understand that a whole lot more than pushing with your hands or kneeing with your legs. These tend to excite, where quiet ignoring and body turning has a much better and long-lasting effect. Just be patient. Learning this way takes time, but dogs will retain the lesson once learned if everyone is consistent and rewards come when appropriate behavior is performed.

You may ask what was so wrong with little Miss Merry jumping into my human's lap? She's small, cuddly, and oh so adorable. Well, there's nothing wrong with dogs sitting on their human's lap…when they are invited. When dogs decide to do something, like jumping on a human's lap, it often puts them in the leader position—they have made a decision for what they want, and they go after it. Granted there are some peaceful, lovable dogs who have no desire to lead and can jump on a couch with ne'er a thought in their minds of staging a coup. However, there are other dogs, like Merry, who view themselves as the spoiled princess of the house. When dogs like Merry jump on a couch (also bed, chair, or any comfortable place intended for humans) uninvited, they often view their throne as theirs and theirs alone. These dogs will growl at anyone coming near or those attempting to dethrone them. Dogs who have this "royal" attitude need to be taught a few rules. By teaching them to ask before being allowed on the couch, the human is showing the dog that the leader chooses who gets to sit (or sleep) on the prime spots.

Being a good leader takes a lot of work (which is why most dogs would rather not have the job unless forced to because no one else will take the lead). Leading a dog doesn't happen in just the few situations I mentioned. It's an all day job. Every time you interact with your dog, you are showing your leadership. If your dog approaches, ask for a sit before you pet your dog. If your dog pushes at your hand and insists on petting, ignore the dog. Don't allow dogs to demand your attention—teach them how to politely elicit your attention by sitting next to you or lying at your feet. When you give your dog a treat, ask for some type of action first—a sit, down, stay, or a fun trick. If your dog begs at the table, don't give the dog food. Ignore the dog. If the dog goes and lies down, thank the dog softly and go on eating. Feeding the dog at the table will only lead to begging. If you give into begging, your dog is leading you, not the other way around. Is that what you want? It may seem like minor situations, but all added together can lead to living with a pretty bossy dog, which also means a potential for growling and biting.

I've heard people tell my human that they don't want to make their dog work for everything, but I don't look at it as work. I love attention from my human. When she asks me to do a spin, shake hands, or a go into a down, I want to do it to show her how clever I am and win that prize. (A word of caution: When asking a St. Bernard to spin, make sure there is plenty of space and nothing breakable on the coffee table. Our tails are deadly to trinkets and drinks!) Doing things for my human is all part of a fun game which gets attention from my human—my leader, my companion, my friend.

Paws to Ponder

Leaders stand tall, give clear instructions through body language, use only verbal cues the dog has been taught, and give plenty of incentives. Anyone, any size in the family can be a positive leader. Leaders are not bullies who lead by sheer force. Leaders calmly guide the team with mutual respect for all members. Just as in the childhood game of "Follow the Leader," make leading your dog a fun game, and she will happily follow.

Chapter  3

The Verbal World
of Humans

The Verbal World of Humans

Dogs are visual; humans are verbal. Our relationship starts with a big communication gap. Dogs are capable of learning human words if you take the time to teach us to understand what we are hearing. Some dogs can learn a lot of words (around 300 have been recorded with some dogs). Other dogs can only learn around 60. The key in communicating with your dog is not always what you say, but how you say it. The intonation of voice means much more to a dog than the actual words. That's not to say that we can't learn individual words, but we learn faster if you pay attention to *how* you say the words and avoid excessive talking.

Here are a few humans I have observed over the years while sitting in on dog training classes. It's enough to make a dog chuckle and shake her head to see so many faux paws (yes, that was intentional) made by humans. If they only knew! I've used the names I've given each person to protect the innocent, and because I don't know their real names.

Mr. Monotone talked to his dog all in one tone of voice. When he wanted his dog to come he said, "c-o-m-e f-i-d-o," all in one tone as if it were one word. Guess what? Fido wouldn't come.

Mrs. Excitable chattered to her dog in a high pitch voice. "Come on boy. Yeah, you can do it boy. Woohoo, come on, come on, come on." Her dog came with such enthusiasm, he knocked her over on arrival.

Mr. Shiny-head yelled all his commands to his dog. "FIDO, COME NOW!" Fido wouldn't come and cowered on the other side of the room.

Miss Sweetie-Pie calmly talked to her dog, begging him to come. "Oh my little darling, don't you want to come to mama? I love your cutie face so much, and I just want to give you a great big hug." The dog sat confused at all the words not sure if he should come or not. He also remembered being mugged by hugs the last time he came—not always incentive for a dog to repeat a behavior.

Although the personalities of these people greatly differed, they had a lot in common. They all loved their dogs, had fun with their dogs, wanted their dogs to share their lives and their homes, and they all were equally frustrated with their dogs. They weren't getting the response they wanted, because they didn't understand the needs of their dogs who also had differing personalities.

Some dogs, like Mr. Monotone's Mastiff, needed a happier voice to achieve motivation; others like Mrs. Excitable's Border Collie required a calmer voice to bring down the energy level. Mr. Shiny-head mistakenly felt it necessary to shout orders at his dog to show his authority, which just turned his poor shy Sheltie mix into a quivering bowl of jelly. Miss Sweetie-Pie talked too much to her Cocker and didn't give him the clear and concise instructions he needed. She also rewarded him with hugs—most dogs do not enjoy hugs, although many learn to tolerate them for their human's sake.

Dogs tend to respond to a "happy" tone of voice. It's part of the game. Dogs learn what different intonations mean in the human world. A happy voice indicates our humans are in a good mood and that means they will often play or give treats. A loud booming voice means our humans are in a foul mood and will most likely ignore dogs, push them out of the way, or worse.

Dogs usually respond with tail wags to the happy voice, and tail tucks or growls to the loud voice. We don't necessarily connect the loud voice with any action of our own; we just know bad things happen when that voice is heard. This is where a lot of misunderstanding comes into play between dogs and humans. Humans think they are punishing us and that we understand by our reaction, but actually quite the opposite may be happening. We are responding to our human's mood, not any action that we may have performed earlier.

Here's an example:

Little Molly was a 12-week-old puppy. She squatted and peed on the expensive oriental carpet right in front of her human. Her human yelled, grabbed Molly by the scruff of her neck, and rubbed Molly's nose in it, while saying, "Bad dog." Molly's human felt she taught Molly that she should not pee inside the house. On the contrary, poor little Molly only thought, "Wow, I better not pee in front of her again; she goes crazy when I pee." From that day on, when Molly's human took her for a walk and waited for her to pee, Molly held it. She remembered—"Don't pee in front of the psychotic human." Molly always held her bursting bladder until they returned home where Molly would instantly run behind the couch and relieve herself.

Molly's human yelled and isolated Molly in her crate. Molly's human was confused and frustrated. Molly was confused and frustrated. Molly knew she needed to relieve her bladder, but she didn't understand where she could go to make her human happy.

All her human did was yell at Molly for relieving herself inside. Instead her human could have interrupted Molly's peeing on the rug with an "Oops," and redirected her outside to finish her business at which time she could then give Molly praise and a little treat for doing her business in the proper place. Molly then would start to make the connection and realize if she peed inside on the rug, she'd be interrupted and brought outside where her human became happy and rewarded her for a job well-done. Molly would repeat the latter behavior because she would receive screeches of delight instead of anguish. (For more on housebreaking, read—what else?—the *Housebreaking Chapter.*)

Paws to Ponder

Angry voices discourage a dog. Happy voices are more rewarding. It's not the words you say that matter when talking to your dog; it's the tone of voice. If you have an excited dog, keep your voice happy but calm. If you have a lazy dog, get excited and happy to encourage your dog. If you are angry, say whatever you want to release your anger, but say it in a happy way!

Chapter 4

Say What You Want

"Delilah!"

My name was said in a sing song way. I heard it and wagged my tail.

"Delilah!"

This time my name was said quicker, and again I wagged my tail.

"DE-LI-LAAH!"

This time it was a shout. I froze and didn't wag my tail. Something was amiss.

"I know you hear me because you wagged your tail!" The voice was no longer happy. It was like a screech the crows make high in the trees.

I wasn't sure what the screeching woman wanted. Yes, of course I heard my name called. I'm a dog and have a great sense of hearing. I heard the name the first time and wagged my tail in acknowledgement, what more did she want from me? The door slammed, and I continued to sniff where squirrels once foraged in the yard. The door opened again, and I continued to sniff. I heard the woman talking. I turned to see who was there with her, but she only held that thing to her ear that makes people talk to themselves.

"YOUR dog is stubborn and refuses to come when I call," she said in her angry, you-better-not-come-near-me-I'm-psychotic-voice. I had heard that voice before and knew it was not in my best interest to be near her when she was in that mood.

"I've called and called for her, but she refuses to budge," she continued as her voice rose higher in pitch with each word—yet another cue that I should stay far away. "I told you we should get rid of this horrible beast. She's nothing but a nuisance." She slammed down the thing she had held to her ear, and stomped out into the yard. Her body leaned forward as she stared at me. Her teeth bared and not in that friendly kind of smiling way humans do sometimes. I tried to decide if I should run or cower. I decided to cower and show her I meant her no harm.

"Yeah, you know you are in trouble, you bad, bad dog. Look at you feeling so guilty. Shame, shame, shame on you for not listening to me when I called. What am I going to do with you? I can't come running out here every time I need you to get your behind in the house. You are a baaaad dog."

The words sounded like "blah-blah-blah" to me. All I knew was she was angry—very angry. Someone must have really put her in a foul mood. I just kept showing her submission by cowering so she'd let go of the tight grip she had on my collar. Finally, she did and I made a break for it. Instantly I ran to the comfort and safety of my crate.

"You know how bad you are. Look, you even went to time-out in your crate on your own."

She really was in a bad mood. Phew, at least I was safe in my cozy crate. If only I possessed opposable thumbs in order to close the gate! I sat and wondered what happened. One minute I was tracking squirrels, and the next minute the world was caving in on me.

Let's take a look at this scenario. I was out having a good 'ol time in the yard when my name was called. I wagged my tail in acknowledgement. Not once did anyone say I was supposed to do something. Only my name was called—no instruction on what was desired next. How are dogs to know what a human wants of them if no further instruction follows, or if we are not taught what behavior is expected when a our name is called?

The woman's voice got louder and louder as she talked to that gadget to her ear. Dogs may have experienced a human's wrath before, and when they hear an angry voice, they will either run (the flight instinct is high in dogs, most of us don't want confrontation), assume a submissive position (in the hopes that we can calm the situation and show we mean no harm) or, heaven-forbid, bite or growl at the human who is approaching in a threatening manner (if the dog has a high sense of self-protection or feels trapped and can't run, this may happen).

Now say a person actually gives an instruction to a dog after calling his

26

name, but the dog doesn't respond. This makes me question whether the dog is stubborn or if the person actually took time to teach what those instructions mean and in all situations? After all, choosing between smelling a squirrel and going to your human is a tough choice. If this skill has not been practiced with distractions, some dogs may not know they are supposed to respond. Then there are some dogs who may ignore instructions not because they are stubborn, but because they genetically have been designed to stay focused on certain tasks. For example, my friend Lucky the beagle doesn't seem to hear anything when chasing a squirrel. He was bred to sniff out prey and hunt it down no matter what the obstacle. The rest of us will come running when called, because we have been taught the benefits to answering the "Come" call. Lucky stays in fast pursuit of the squirrel because his brain has tuned out the rest of the world. Personally, the biscuit I receive when I go to my human is a far safer bet than me catching that squirrel, but most beagles can't see (or hear) beyond the lovely scent of a critter on the run.

Humans can be the same way. Be honest, how many of you humans hear your significant other call, but turn a deaf ear because you are distracted by something else—perhaps football or when you are chatting with a friend? This is one aspect we dogs and humans have in common. When we are distracted, it's difficult to drop everything and come running unless we feel it is in our best interest to do so. Depending on the distraction level, the reward for listening might have to be very high quality—steak inspires me to listen!

Humans mistakenly think that when a puppy happily follows them around at four months of age and comes when her name is called that the dog understands what the word "Come" means. All most puppies understand at this stage is this person is responsible for their care; therefore, it's crucial not to let that person out of sight. Once the puppy discovers there is a big world out there just waiting to be explored (often in the fifth month of life), the human becomes less interesting, and the world becomes a wonderful playground. Feeling quite hurt, the human takes this ignoring personally and gets frustrated. All it takes is some more training to overcome this problem.

It's crucial that people take the time to teach a dog what certain words

27

in the human-language mean and then use those words in a lot of different situations so the dog knows what behavior is desired. That doesn't mean using the word just a few times and then assuming the dog knows the word. Learning a foreign language is tough. It's even tougher if you are a species who relies more on non-verbal than verbal communication. Training needs to take place regularly over a period of time—start in a quiet location and build up to many distractions and more distance between the human and dog. It takes patience, consistency, and lots of love and praise.

 Paws to Ponder

Calling a dog's name does not tell the dog what you want her to do next. You may want to teach the dog to look at you when her name is said or use a "Look" cue. Dogs, like people, listen better when they are making eye contact. Once you have your dog's attention, then direct the dog with other cues your dog has been taught. See the chapter on *The Basics* for more on how to teach basic skills such as "Look," "Come," and much more.

Chapter **5**

Will Work
for
Food

Will Work for Food

I love food. I would love to be fed all day long. However, I hear it's not healthy to gain too much weight, especially for a big dog like me. It's up to my human to monitor my food intake and make sure I'm the proper size to stay healthy. Twice a day I'm fed a certain amount of high-quality food based on my size and energy level. I get a little less in the summer, because it's too hot for me to run around and a little more in the winter, when I'm active. (This may be different for other dogs; I just don't like the heat since I was bred for colder weather.) The food is not left out all day for me to eat for a few reasons. One, I might eat more than I should. Two, we have multiple dogs in the house so other dogs might eat my food, which may cause them to get fat, or fights may occur over food. Three, by managing when I get food, my human is showing me that she is in charge of my most important resource—food. Dogs know they need food to survive, so we tend to listen to the person in charge of the stuff.

In training, my human uses food in the beginning to help teach dogs how to behave in a human world. I thought this was the best game ever! I do something she wants; I get a treat or some of my food. Sweet deal! Figuring out what my human wants isn't always easy. Sometimes she let's me figure it out for myself. I'll try different actions, and finally she'll say "Yes" to one and give me a treat. I then repeat that action, because I realize a treat comes afterwards. Once the action is refined, it gets a name. It's called shaping, but I really don't care what it's called. I just like the game.

The other way my human taught me proper manners was by guiding me with the treat. To learn a down, she put the treat in front of my nose and lured me down to the ground. When I went down with my front paws, I got a "Yes" and a treat. Eventually I learned the word "Down" means to lie on the floor.

Treats are really cool, and I like them a lot, but it's important to fade the treats from your training program if you really want your dog to listen all the time. Otherwise, you will end up with a dog who holds a sign that says "Will Work For Food," and you will always have to have treats in your pocket to get your dog to listen. The first time I did something and didn't get a treat, I looked at my human and thought, "Hey, where's my treat. All I get is a 'Good'? What's up with that?" So I tried the action again. I got a "Yes" and a treat.

"That's more like it," I thought. I repeated the action. No treat. I repeated it again. No treat. I repeated it again. I got a "Yes" and a treat. After a while I caught on to this new game. I repeated behaviors asked of me and eventually a reward was given. Now I had to really listen, so that I didn't miss out on that treat. I had no idea when it was coming, so I became even more attentive to my human.

After a while, my human no longer carried the treat bag with her. She put it over on a shelf in the room and asked me to do a series of moves. Then she said, "Yay, treat time," and we'd walk over to the shelf to get my reward. If I walked over during training and looked at the shelf with the treats, my human would just turn her back and stand in the middle of the room ignoring me. When I walked back to her, she'd get all happy; we did more training and then went to the treat shelf together. I learned that SHE chose when I got a treat, not me.

When dogs get into the "Will Work for Food" mode, the only time they will listen to their human is if there is food in the human's hand. People get very frustrated with their dogs when this happens. They complain that the dog ignores them when no food is around or becomes demanding that food be given every second. That's because they haven't faded the food properly in training. When my human calls me while I'm barking at the killer squirrels outside our fence, I come running at the chance I may get a reward. Usually when I'm really involved in something and come when called, I'm more likely to get some kind of goody. I've learned it behooves me to leave the squirrels for another day and listen to my human's call. When food is either suddenly stopped or always there, the incentive to listen isn't as great.

Look at it this way. People go to work because they need money. They don't get paid every day, but they go back to work because they know the money is coming at some point. If the boss suddenly stopped paying all together, most likely people would stop going to work. Dogs work for their humans because they know the pay is coming at some point. Don't totally eliminate rewards; however, if you give a reward for every single task, you may end up with a dog that holds up a "Will Work for Food" sign.

NOTE: Food is not the only reward available to dogs. I like to play with toys, sniff, and get scratches behind my ear and on my belly. Depending on my mood, any one of those things could be considered a reward. Look for every day rewards for your dog. Don't just put that food bowl down, have the dog sit and stay and then reward by putting the food down. Better yet, make the dog work for all food during the day instead of eating out of a bowl. He who controls the food, controls the dog. It's not cruel to your dog. I really enjoy the extra attention while I do different tasks to earn my food. If the dog wants to play ball, have the dog work on a few cue words first, and then reward the dog by throwing the ball. Dogs won't hold up the "Will Work for Food" sign if you vary rewards, so take the time to find out what else inspires your dog to listen and respond. Once you figure out what inspires your dog, you are ready to go on to the next chapter to learn how to teach some basic cues.

Paws to Ponder

Fading the food from training is a gradual procedure. A variable reward schedule is important since dogs are great at figuring out routines. If you give the treat every third time, you're likely to have a dog who will only perform every third request. Mix things up while you fade the food so your dog doesn't know what's coming next.

Don't give a dog a treat every time they come in the house. Not only does this lessen the chances of getting a reliable recall when there are distractions (the treat is always there so why bother?), but it can create a demanding (and fat) dog. Keep 'em guessing, so they'll keep on responding to your requests.

Chapter 6

Teach

What you Want:

The Basics

 Paws to Ponder

English is a second language for dogs. Be sure to take the time to teach dogs the meaning of the words you use.

Teach What You Want: The Basics

I've noticed in the human world that there are basic words that all dogs should learn in order to better understand their verbal-based humans. These words are: "Look, Touch, Sit, Down, Stay, Come, Let's go (or some other word that means walk nicely), and Leave it." If a dog learns nothing else, these words will make their life a lot easier when it comes to understanding what humans want. Remember English is a second language for dogs. We don't know the words unless you teach them to us, and if you don't keep practicing, we may forget them.

Dogs learn in a lot of different ways, I know because each family that I was passed to used a different method. One family used a correction collar. When I didn't do what they wanted, they jerked quickly on the collar until I got it right. Sometimes I didn't know what they wanted, so I tried different things until they stopped jerking. It was very stressful, but I eventually figured out what to do to keep them from jerking on the collar. Another family used a shock method of training. I never really understood what they wanted, so I began to cower or just learned to endure the shock (as in the case of my fence jumping). One family hit me occasionally and used loud yells whenever I did something I wasn't supposed to do. It was hard to figure out what they wanted, and I eventually stopped doing a lot of things just to be on the safe side. I became extremely sensitive to loud noises and voices. My current family used treats to lure me into position for some basic skills, and some skills they just captured when I did it (gave me treats when I did something really cute or good and then eventually put a cue word to it).

I found out how much fun learning can be when it's a game. It took a while for me to open up and be a little more cheerful about learning because of my past experiences, but once I figured out what the game was all about, I learned quickly. The steps on the following pages use luring to teach the skills. If your dog struggles with any step, you may want to consider capturing it instead. For instance if the dog is hesitant to lie down, you could wait for the dog to get tired, lie down, and then mark the behavior with a "Yes" (more on how to mark desired behaviors in a moment) and reward it instead of luring the dog into position. Training should be fun, so find a way to teach what you want that makes it fun for both of you. Once basic skills are taught and used, they will stick with your dog for a long time to come, making your relationship with your dog that much better. (Be sure to only use food to lure in the beginning and fade it from training quickly so your dog doesn't become dependent on having food present to perform a task. For more on this, read the chapter entitled *Will Work for Food*.)

Methods to Help Your Dog Learn

Capturing: Wait for the dog to perform a desired task and reward

Luring: Use food to help the dog move into the desired position and reward

Introducing the Marker—The Very First Step

A marker is a sound that tells the dog the action just done was exactly what you wanted and a reward is on its way. A quick sound such as a clicker or a word like "Yes" helps define the action in the dog's mind. If I ask you to jump, the moment you lift yourself into the air, I would say "Yes" and then give you a treat when you landed. This would increase the likelihood that you will want to jump again (provided the treat is something you like). It's the same with your dog, but your dog will not understand what "Jump" means, because he doesn't speak English. First you have to get the dog to do the action, sometimes by luring. We are going to use the marker to let the dog know the moment she does the desired action, and then add the cue word as the action is learned.

The Marker

1. This exercise should be done quietly without excessive talking. (Remember too many words distract.)

2. Choose either a clicker or use the word "Yes" to mark behaviors. In these instructions I will use the word "Yes." If you choose to use a clicker, just click at the same time the instructions indicate "Yes."

3. Show the dog a treat. Say "Yes" and give the dog the treat. Note: the dog does not have to do anything at this point. Just say "Yes" and give a treat.

4. Repeat this several times. Say "Yes" and give a treat. Say "Yes" and give a treat.

Pretty soon your dog will think this is a really cool game and learn that "Yes" means a promise of a reward.

Touch

There are times that human hands can be a scary thing. Many dogs shy away from a hand being thrust in front of their nose. It doesn't necessarily mean they were beaten; it just may be that the sudden movement startled them. Remember the example of the approaching man in the first chapter? The person's hand being thrust in front of the dog caused fear. This fear could be based either in past experience or lack of experience.

People reach out and touch dogs all the time. Whether it's to let dogs sniff their hand, pet them to say hello, grab the collar to hook on a leash, or doing an exam, dogs are touched often. It's crucial for your dog to understand that a hand coming towards her is a good thing. This is often overlooked in most dogs' training repertoire, yet it is something that dogs encounter on a daily basis. If you take your dog for a walk and a child runs up to pet your dog, you want to know your dog will be happy to see the child's extended hand. Granted everyone should always ask if they can pet your dog first, but not every human in the world is well educated on this rule. I had a little boy run up to me and give me a big kiss right on my nose before my human could stop him. Lucky for him, I'm a nice dog, or he might not have a face anymore. It's best to take precautions and train your dog to be wonderful in every situation.

Teaching your dog to touch a hand desensitizes her to a hand coming down towards the dog's face. The touch is also helpful in getting the dog to walk loosely on a leash instead of pulling, and to eventually work further and further away from you. If you want to go on to teach your dog tricks, touch is the precursor to many cool ones—like closing doors, turning on lights, or spinning.

Notice in the picture that I'm not sitting while doing the touch. All I have to do is touch Cheryl's hand. Take a break and give this a try. It's fun and easy! Step-by-step instructions are on the next page.

Touch Cont.

1. Hold your hand out in front of the dog (not touching but close to the dog's face) and wait for the dog to touch your hand with her nose. Don't cheat and bring your hand to the dog's nose. Most of the time, the dog will be curious and automatically sniff your hand.

Note:

Always start out practicing new skills in a quiet environment without distractions. It's easier for us to focus on what you want us to learn. Once your dog is doing well, slowly add distractions. Training doesn't stop just because your dog does well in your living room. Try getting out into the real world and start all over with noises, people, etc. Build distractions slowly so your dog doesn't become overwhelmed.

2. Say "Yes" when the dog shows any curiosity about your hand and give a treat. If the dog is hesitant to touch your hand at all, rub a little peanut butter or cheese on it, but fade this very quickly from the training process.

3. Repeat several times, presenting your hand and waiting for the dog to touch it. Say "Yes" immediately and give a treat.

4. Once the dog is touching your hand repeatedly, add the word "Touch" and then present your hand.

5. Move your hand into different positions around your body and say "Touch." The dog should follow the hand and touch it no matter where you place it. Don't forget to say "Yes" and give the dog a treat when the dog touches your hand.

6. Practice with another person presenting their hand, and you say "Touch." This will help your dog with appropriate greetings. Now a hand coming towards her won't be so scary.

Look

Look

1. Have food in your hand and put it in front of the dog's nose.

2. Move your hand up to your face. When the dog looks up at the food, say "Yes" and give a treat.

3. Repeat this several times.

4. Add the cue "Look" or "Watch" then move the food to your eye. Say "Yes" and then treat when the dog looks at you. Be sure to choose a word and stick with it.

5. Repeat, repeat, repeat.

6. Next put the food in the other hand. Put your empty hand in front of the dog's nose and bring it to your eye, saying the cue word.

7. When the dog follows the empty hand up to your face making eye contact, say "Yes" and treat with the food you are holding in the *other* hand.

8. Once you've repeated all this many times, start to eliminate the movement of your hand to your eye and just say the cue word. Change between the hand signal and cue so the dog learns both.

9. Now try it with distractions. Start with really yummy food and use the hand signal again when first adding distractions. Then fade the food. Distractions add a new factor to learning, so you may feel like you are starting at step one which is perfectly normal.

Getting your dog to look at you before giving instructions for what you want next will help a dog become a better listener. In the dog world, eye contact means a challenge. In this case, you are teaching the dog that eye contact with you means good things happen. You can use this to get your dog's focus on you prior to training or when you need the dog to turn his focus away from a certain situation, i.e. a dog passing by, or a squirrel climbing a tree.

Sit

Sit

Sit is usually a simple and definitely useful skill for all dogs to know. It can be used in many situations, i.e. greetings, receiving treats or food, waiting for attention, putting on a leash, playing games, at the veterinarian's office—the list is endless.

1. Hold a treat in your hand. Stand in front of the dog. Place your hand in front of the dog's nose.

If your dog struggles with sitting on cue, try capturing—waiting for the dog to sit during the normal course of the day and then reward. If that doesn't work, teach a down first, and then try to get your dog to back up from a down into a sit. Sometimes training takes a little creativity.

2. Move your hand slowly, keeping it close to the dog's nose, as you move it in a flowing motion up over the dog's nose and then head. This will cause the dog to follow the treat and put his bottom on the floor. Don't put your hand too high or the dog will jump for the treat. As soon as the dog's bottom hits the floor, say "Yes" and give the treat.

3. Repeat, repeat, repeat. If your dog backs up instead of sitting, work in a corner.

4. Add the word when the dog starts to sit reliably using the steps above. Say "Sit" prior to moving the treat over the dog's head. Say "Sit" only once. When the dog's bottom hits the ground, say "Yes" and follow with a treat.

5. Once the dog starts sitting regularly stop luring with your hand over the dog's head and hold your hand at waist height. Also try turning your back to the dog and say "Sit." This is a good test to see if the dog really knows the cue word.

6. Use food intermittently as a reward when the dog begins to understand "Sit." Eventually the dog should perform several tasks in a row before getting a treat. Build up to this slowly, though.

Show the dog the treat.

Bring your hand up over the dog's head. Dog's bottom will usually go down while she tries to follow the treat with her nose.

Say "Yes" the moment the dog's bottom hits the ground.
Give the treat.
YUM!

Note: Add the cue word sit any time, but say "Sit" only once. Saying "Sit, sit, sit" over and over again does not help a dog learn to sit any faster. It would be like me saying "Ruff, ruff, ruff," and expecting you to know what that means. You don't understand my "Ruff" anymore than a dog understands your "Sit" until you help the dog make the connection. If you say "Sit" repeatedly, the dog may think the word for "Sit" is actually "Sitsitsitsit" and wait until you finish the word before sitting. Stick to just saying the word once and be patient and wait for the dog to sit.

Come

Come

1. Have the dog sit in front of you. Be sure to have a leash on your dog for control.

2. Hold a treat in front of the dog's nose and start to back away from the dog. As the dog moves with you, say "Yes" and give the treat. *(Note: You are teaching "Come"—the dog does not have to stay as you move. You want the dog to come with you. Teaching "Stay" is later.)*

3. Repeat. If the dog is hesitant to come directly to you, put the treat behind your back and turn around luring the dog to move with you as you walk away. Some shy dogs are less hesitant with your back turned since a face staring at them can be threatening.

Come is such an important cue for every dog to know as it could save your dog's life. It's important to start teaching in a distraction-free environment and then build to more and more distractions and longer distances away from your dog. Dogs get confused easily, so don't add distractions and distance together. Build each separately, and be patient. Also note that off-leash work takes time to build up to. Do not expect your dog to respond off-leash when first teaching this cue. These are only the basic first steps.

4. Once the dog is reliably coming as you move, add the word "Come" before you start to back up.

5. Add a sit at the end of the come by moving your hand quickly up to your waist when you stop. Stand straight as the dog comes closer to you. This should encourage the dog to sit as he looks up at you. If necessary, give the "Sit" cue. After the dog comes to you and sits, remember to say "Yes" and give a treat.

6. Don't use the cue "Come" in other situations if you feel your dog will not listen. Using the cue without requiring a dog to respond will make the dog believe this is an optional task.

Show the dog the treat, say the dog's name, and start moving backwards.

Keep moving back. Just a few steps. Don't go too far in the beginning or the dog may not come straight in.

Stop and bring the treat up to your chest.

The dog will sit while looking at the treat. Reward.

Notice my reward is being withheld in the last picture despite the sit. That's because I was barking. Cheryl waited to reward me when I was quiet. Otherwise I would learn that come means "Come, Sit, Bark"—Not what you want to encourage!

Down

Down is a great word to help dogs learn to settle for a while. It's a comfortable position to be in and helps a dog learn to relax. Some dogs do not like this position as they feel more vulnerable, especially if they are in an uncomfortable atmosphere or around unfamiliar people, so start teaching this in a quiet, familiar area. Don't push on your dog to try to get her to go down. Dogs tend to be more resistant when being forced into position, plus pushing on a dog's hips may cause joint problems. Be patient and help the dog learn what you want through luring, or capturing, but not pushing.

Down

1. Start the dog in a sit or stand. Put your right hand with a treat in it in front of your dog's nose and bring it slowly down to the ground.

3. Turn the palm of your hand down so that the food is between your hand and the ground.

4. Say "Yes" when the dog follows the treat into a down position and give the treat.

5. If a dog is resistant, say "Yes" as soon as the dog starts to extend his legs forward into the down position and give the treat. After the dog does this a few times, try to get the dog to move the front legs further down each time.

6. If the dog puts the front end down and the rear end rises (like a see-saw) try moving your hand slower or bringing the dog down under something low—either a low table, chair, or get on the floor and bring the dog under your legs. When the dog lies all the way down (elbows touching and rear on the ground), say "Yes" and give the treat. Repeat, repeat, repeat.

7. Say the word "Down" prior to luring the dog with your hand.

9. Fade the food from your hand as the dog becomes proficient, and start to go only part way to the floor with your hand. Try using the word without the hand signal to see if the dog understands.

Start from a sit or a stand. Show the dog the treat.

Bring the treat down to the floor. Reward any moves to go down, i.e. movement of the front paw.

Continue to move your hand down towards the ground. Be sure not to move your hand forward or the dog might get up.

Once the dog goes all the way down, say "Yes" and reward. No cheating—elbows should be on the ground for a full down.

Some dogs aren't sure what you want when teaching a down. If this is the case, make a bridge with your knees or work with a low table or chair.

Get the dog's attention and show the treat under your leg.

Have the dog follow the treat under your leg. Say "Yes" and treat any movement to lie down. Repeat. Soon the dog will get what "Down" means and won't need to go under something.

Sometimes dogs get a little goofy during training. If this happens at inappropriate times, ignore the behavior, wait for the dog to return to you, or lure with a treat. If your dog continues this behavior, it could be a sign that the dog is stressed with the training, and it's time for a break.

Note: If you have a dog who is resistant to learning "Down," capture it. This means waiting and watching, and when your dog gets bored and lies down, say "Yes" and give the dog a treat. Continue to do this and watch the downs increase as the dog catches on to what you desire.

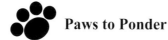 **Paws to Ponder**

The words used as cues are just an example. Pick any word, but be consistent. Everyone interacting with the dog should use the same words. Hand signals are useful when you want to silently lead your dog. The movement made while luring your dog becomes the hand signal. For example, "Look" = bring your hand to your eye. "Down" = moving your hand in a downward manner. Switching between hand and word cues will allow your dog to learn and retain both meanings.

Stay

Stay is a wonderful skill to teach your dog so he won't move from a particular spot. A stay is useful if you go someplace with your dog and need him to stay in one spot while eating in an outdoor cafe, or if you have company, and you don't want your dog interacting with the person. (Some people don't like dogs, although I totally can't understand why—we are soooo lovable. What harm is a little slobber and fur on your clothes?)

One of the biggest mistakes I see people make when teaching "Stay" is they combine it with "Come" every time they use it. Dogs chain cues together. If you always ask us to "Sit" and then "Down," pretty soon you will have a dog who does a sit and then a down every time you say "Sit." The same is true of the cues "Stay" and "Come." If you always say "Stay" and then use "Come," soon your dog will think, "Oh, I know what's next," and get up breaking the stay and proudly coming to you. The dog is confused when the human gets frustrated at what the dog felt was very clever indeed.

Vary the order of training to keep your dog guessing. When teaching "Stay," start by only going to your dog when the stay is over instead of calling your dog to you. That way the dog gets used to you approaching, which may come in handy if you need to go to your dog and attach a leash. When you progress to using "Come" in conjunction with "Stay," mix it up. If we can't anticipate your next cue, we'll learn to wait and listen to what you say—provided you don't make us wait too long. Some breeds aren't known for their patience!

A solid "Stay" is important to keep your dog safe, so take the time to teach it correctly from the beginning. Going back and retraining is so much harder than doing it right the first time. If your dog struggles with holding still, start out with your dog on a leash and wait for the dog to settle. Say "Yes" and reward the settle. This helps excitable dogs learn to go from zany to zen and sets the stage for learning a more reliable "Stay."

Stay

1. Eliminate any distractions, especially moving objects, prior to starting on this skill.

2. Place the dog in a sit position at your left side.

Note: Be sure to use the word "Stay" only when you want the dog to stay in one place. When you leave the house to go somewhere, you do not want to confuse a dog by saying "Stay." Use another cue such as "Wait here" or "Good-bye."

3. Say the word "Stay," putting your hand in front of the dog's nose.

4. Put your hand back at waist height and then take a step with your right leg (the leg away from the dog) and step right in front of the dog so you are facing him.

5. Before the dog moves, step back to the original position say "Yes" and give him a treat.

6. Repeat these steps a few times, so he'll get the idea that "Stay" means he stays while you move.

7. Begin to increase the distance you move away from the dog to two, three, and four steps. Do not increase distance until the dog is staying at the shorter distances. Return to the dog each time and reward and praise. (Once the dog is doing reliable stays, you can add "Come" *every once in a while*. Don't do it all the time or the dog will start to come automatically after you say "Stay.")

8. Add distractions as the dog learns to stay reliably. You may need to decrease the distance when you add distractions. Learning a stay with distractions is a whole new trick. It's tough to stay when a cute little Poodle struts by!

Stay

Sit the dog at your left side.

Put a hand in front of your dog's face, say "Stay," and then move in front of your dog. In the beginning you may need to keep your hand in front of the dog's face in order to help the dog stay still.

Once the dog gets used to you moving back and forth from the side position to the front, start to take just a baby step backward. Remind the dog to "Staaay." Do not have a treat in your hand or the dog will follow it!

Hand signals help remind us what you want since in the beginning the cue word really doesn't mean much to us. Here Cheryl reminds me that I'm supposed to stay in place, because she sees I'm getting excited which increases the likelihood that I will move.

As the dog begins to understand the concept of stay, add duration (the amount of time the dog sits in a stay) slowly. Don't add distance and duration at the same time. Gradually step things up to set the dog up for success.

Test how well your dog understands "Stay" by turning your back. Some dogs will only stay put when they are making eye contact with their human. You want to eventually work up to being able to leave the room, so this is a good way to start.

Leave It

Leave It

Note: If your dog has food aggression issues, contact a behaviorist immediately before proceeding with this exercise.

Learning to leave something alone is helpful when your dog finds something that may be dangerous or is a distraction. It is taught with food but can be used with anything you want your dog to leave alone after the behavior is learned, i.e. cats, squirrels, off limit items in the house, food dropped on the floor.

1. Hold a piece of food inside your closed hand in front of your dog's nose.

2. Tell your dog "Leave it" as your dog reaches to try to get the food. Pull the food away slightly.

3. Repeat this step until the dog finally ignores the food (usually out of frustration at first).

4. Say "Yes" and give the dog a treat from your other hand.

5. Repeat steps 1 – 4 slowly increasing the time that the dog has to look away from your hand with the food. (Looking away teaches proper body language if you use this to leave another dog alone.)

6. Now begin to open your hand, a little at a time, as the food is placed in front of the dog and say "Leave It." (If the dog continually reaches for the food, giving an "Eh" sound instead of repeating the cue is more successful.)

7. Try putting the food on the floor in front of your dog. Be ready to cover the food with your hand or foot if the dog reaches for it. If the dog gets the treat, he may begin to think this is a game of who can get the treat first, making your job much harder. Once the dog leaves the treat and looks away, say "Yes" and pick up the treat. Either give the dog the treat from the floor with a cue word that it is all right to eat it, or give a different treat as a reward.

Final Note on Teaching the Basics:

Loose leash walking has a chapter all of its own, since it is such an important skill for dogs to learn. It's one of the more desired skills people want their dogs to learn, but also one of the skills that takes the most time and patience to teach.

Take your time while climbing these basic steps with your dog. Don't rush the process. Some dogs learn quickly. Other dogs need a little more time to catch on. I'm typically a lazy dog, and I don't like to work more than fifteen minutes. If my human tries to work me longer than that I lie down and give up. She's learned to work with me in small increments, so we can always end on a positive note. Oliver, my Poodle friend, loves to learn and can work for an hour or more learning new tasks. I'm not that motivated. It's just too much work for me! Judge what your dog's limits are and work within them so you both have a *fun* learning experience.

Make training a game
and keep it fun for all
involved.

Chapter **7**

Putting
the Basics
Into Action

Putting the Basics into Action

A h, I remember how excited everyone in our house was when they mentioned "The Grandparents" were coming. All members of the household were scurrying around. They spent days vacuuming, dusting, and cleaning up the yard for "The Grandparents." I followed my humans around watching with anticipation wondering just what "The Grandparents" were all about. Then the family turned and looked at me.

"What are we going to do about Delilah?" One of them asked. "She's bound to knock over Grandma with her enthusiasm."

"Yes, and remember last Thanksgiving when she took the cheese ball off the table when no one was looking? Grandma would have a fit if she did that in front of her!"

Hey, in my defense, no one seemed interested in the cheese ball, and it was right there on the edge of the table, nose height. *Anyway*…the conversation continued.

"Maybe we should send her to the kennel while "The Grandparents" are here."

That didn't sound like any fun at all. I didn't want to go to the kennel. Then I'd never find out what "The Grandparents" were all about, although right at that moment I wasn't fond of "The Grandparents" at all.

"Delilah wouldn't like the kennel. We just need to teach her some manners while Grandma is here." Now that's my kind of thinking. No kennel. Some of my friends like going, but I prefer staying at home with my humans.

"If she hasn't learned any manners by now, she certainly won't be any better in just a few days." I didn't like where this was going.

"Well, we owe it to her to give it a try. She's already got some basic skills, we just have to teach her to use those skills in different situations."

Many times, humans teach their dogs basic skills of sit, down, stay, come, walk on a loose leash, and leave it, but then neglect to teach the dogs when to use those skills. Just because we have been taught what the words mean, does not mean we know when to use the skills to go with the words.

For instance, I know "Sit," but I may not know to sit when "The Grandparents" come in the door, because I haven't been taught to use my sit skill in that situation. It's up to my human to show me that "Sit" is the desired behavior when I greet people. I may know the cue "Down" means to put my body all the way on the floor, but I don't know that I should do that while "The Grandparents" sit and visit. I know the words "Leave it" mean to leave a piece of food when offered, but no one told me those words extended to the cheese ball sitting all alone on the very edge of the table, taunting me with its smell…YUM!

Not only do humans need to take the time to teach their dogs basic skills in order to be well-mannered canines in the human world, they also need to teach us when to use those skills. Dogs don't generalize well, so it may mean teaching the skills in a variety of situations. If I learn to walk on a loose leash in my quiet neighborhood, that doesn't mean I'll walk nicely on a loose leash in a park filled with other dogs and people. If I learn to sit to greet people when they come in the house, that doesn't mean I know to sit to greet people if they come up to me on the street. If I learn to leave my food bowl as it's being placed on the floor for suppertime, that doesn't mean I know to leave the tasty cheese ball sitting on the edge of the table, calling my name.

O.K. so even if I *did* know that food on the table was off-limits, everyone gives into temptation at some point in their life—even humans! Oh, and by the way, when I got caught with the cheese ball, and my human called me over—I did come. (I've been taught to come when called.) I did give the cheese ball to my human. (I've been taught to give items in my mouth.) I was rewarded with a bone to chew instead of the tasty cheese ball, so all turned out fine in the end. The only thing I didn't understand is why my human threw away the cheese ball. If she didn't want it, what was the big deal about me having it??

Sorry, I got off point. Let's see what was the point? Oh, right...

After you have taught us basic skills,
Teach us when to use those skills.

When "The Grandparents" arrived, my humans put a leash on me and asked me to sit to greet. I did. "The Grandparents" were very kind and had a bone for me. I graciously took the bone, went to my settle spot as requested by my humans, did a down, and quietly ate my bone while my humans and "The Grandparents" visited. I really liked "The Grandparents" and am glad I didn't have to go to the kennel. All it took was a little effort on the part of my humans to make sure they showed me the behaviors they wanted. Dogs need guidance to understand what is expected. After all, greeting people at the door can be a pretty exciting experience when all the humans are hugging and talking loudly. What's to keep the dog from jumping around barking, unless you teach us another way to behave?

Oh, and by the way, when my humans put the leash on me and opened the door, they kept their greeting calmer than usual to help me stay calm. Sometimes humans need to change their behavior to help the dog change too.

Paws to Ponder

Teaching your dog the basics is the crucial first step, but training doesn't stop there. Use those basic skills to help your dog learn how to behave in a variety of situations and always, always keep practicing so the dog doesn't get rusty on skills learned. If you don't use them, the dog may lose them.

Chapter 8

These Paws Were Made For Walking

These Paws were Made for Walking

I love going for a walk. Not only is it great exercise, but it's a wonderful time to smell and investigate the neighborhood. Oliver, my little Poodle buddy, loves to stop at every tree, read his pee-mail, and then leave some for other dogs to read. I do it too, but not with the same enthusiasm as Oliver. When he gets outside, he darts hither and yon, pulling on the leash all the way. This seems to be where the problem comes in for many humans. They don't appreciate being pulled down the road by an enthusiastic pee-mail reader.

If walking on a loose leash is so important to humans, why do they allow their dogs to pull down the street? Humans are such baffling creatures! One walk they are being propelled down the road by their dog, doing nothing to stop the behavior; the next time they are yelling at the dog to stop pulling. The dog at the end of the leash has no clue what the human wants, so the dog continues to pull. Walking is very rewarding. If the dog is pulling while walking, the dog is getting rewarded for pulling. Therefore, in the dog's mind, pulling must be an acceptable behavior.

In my house, dogs aren't allowed to walk forward on a leash if they don't walk correctly. I learned to walk in the correct position through a trial and error process. With every step my human took, when I stayed next to her, we continued to walk forward. If I pulled, we stopped. Sometimes we even walked backward, which was very frustrating if there was something I wanted to get that was ahead of me. Step-by-step, inch-by-inch, we worked until I learned to walk without pulling. In the beginning I got little treats for walking in the proper place. A jackpot was earned when I got to our destination walking appropriately. The jackpot was a pile of treats set at the end of our walk, usually placed in sight as we worked on the walking skills. Let me tell you, it's tough not to pull toward a pile of treats, but once I figured out I'd never get to the treats if I pulled, I walked right next to my human. The treats were worth it, but by the heavy sighs of my human, I think she got a little impatient with my learning process.

Humans want instant results, and that doesn't happen, at least not usually with loose leash walking. We are so excited to be outside that we want to pull and sniff and go everywhere. However, once I figured out I could still sniff and enjoy my walk right next to my human, I was happy to stop pulling. Oliver is still working on this skill, and I have to chuckle as I watch my human working with him in the driveway. Sometimes they walk further backward than they do forward! Oliver is slowly getting better—some dogs just take more patience than others, and no dog has tested my human's patience like Oliver!

At no point in our training are the dogs in our family allowed to go for what I've heard called a "fun" walk. This is a walk, according to some humans, that allows the dog to go wherever he wants. All walks can be fun. A controlled walk is fun if the dog is allowed to walk loosely next to the person and to sniff a little here and there. We don't have to run like a crazy dog all over the place to have fun on a walk. Once we learn where to walk properly, and our human is pleased, we are happy to continue to walk in a controlled manner. It usually means longer walks and new places to explore. It also means our humans spend a lot less time yelling, pulling back, and heaving big sighs of exasperation. We are still allowed to stop and read/ leave pee-mail occasionally; we just aren't allowed to pull or stop every two seconds. If we do, that's when our humans should remind us that it's time to keep walking. It's all about compromise. My human knows that sometimes I like to investigate, and I've learned that there are times I need to just keep walking, but pulling is never involved.

This whole controlled fun walk concept seems very difficult for humans to grasp. Many feel they must let their dog pull and run around for the dog to really enjoy a walk. Then they complain when the dog pulls so much it hurts their shoulders and back. I'm confused by this—humans want the dog to have fun running and pulling but want to go for walks where the dog doesn't run and pull. Geez, no wonder dogs can't figure out you humans!

In order for both human and dog to enjoy a walk, it's important for the human to show the dog how and where to walk. Once the dog sees that this is rewarding, the dog will continue to walk in that position. It takes a lot of patience. Don't plan on getting anywhere in the beginning. When I was learning, we did a lot more walking backward than walking forward. Each day, the pulling and walking backward got less and the walking forward came faster. My human is pretty stubborn. She wouldn't give into me pulling at all. To help in the learning process, I was fitted with a head halter. (More on how to use them on page 71.) That thing wasn't my idea of fun at first, since it felt funny on my face, but I had to listen to my human with it on, because now she had gentle control of my head movements. I actually learned faster with the head halter and learned to accept it. Eventually I could go for walks without it. I'm glad my human was persistent, because now we can both take walks and enjoy our time together. She's happy to let me stop and sniff, and I'm happy to walk by her side and not pull.

 Paws to Ponder

It's important to use all training tools properly to avoid hurting a dog. Never jerk on a head halter or allow a dog to run out to the end of the leash while wearing one.

Consistency and patience is the key to loose leash walking. Read through this entire chapter before proceeding with these steps.

1. Get the dog on your left side. (There is no rule about the left side unless you are doing obedience trials; it's just the safer side when walking against traffic. If you prefer that your dog walks on the right, that's fine. Pick a side and stick with it.)

3. Use the "Look" or "Touch" cue to get the dog to pay attention and take a step forward. (See *The Basics* chapter for steps on how to teach these cues.) Say "Yes" and give the dog a treat if the dog steps with you.

4. Repeat taking another step, and continue doing one step at a time slowly. Talk to the dog and try to maintain eye contact.

6. If the dog pulls, stop and wait for the dog to come back and join you. Say "Yes" give a treat, and start walking again. If the dog doesn't return to you when you stop, start walking backward or make a U-turn and walk the other way. When the dog is next to you, turn again and head back the same way. The message to the dog is that he will not make any headway as long as he pulls.

7. Say "Yes" and treat any loose leash walking. Remember this is not a heeling exercise where the dog must stick to your left side by your knee, but a relaxed walk somewhere in the general vicinity of your left side. Do not allow the dog to crisscross in front or behind you. Do not let the dog continually pull on the leash. Dogs will pull harder against a tight leash. If you must pull back on the dog, do so gently and release instantly—slight tugs (not a snap of the leash) and releases are better than a constant tug. However, the ultimate goal is no tugs at all.

9. In the beginning, start training in a distraction-free environment and build up distractions as your dog becomes more proficient. You may have to keep high-power treats with you when walking outside with lots of distractions. Be patient and keep practicing.

Get the dog to look at you and then take a step. Reward the dog every time a step is taken with you.

If the dog pulls ahead, stop. Just stand there.

Don't let the dog get too far ahead. See how the leash isn't let out all the way? The further the dog gets; the less control you have.

Notice Cheryl's pursued lips? She's saying, "Oops" to remind me that I'm not doing the right behavior. That's all she says, and then just waits for me to return. I like the little extra reminder. She does this quietly to help me learn and try another behavior. However, don't repeat words over and over, or we just stop listening.

Praise the dog for returning to you. Notice the nice loose leash again.

Now it's time to take another step. Keep that leash nice and loose and your hand by your side.

Once the dog gets the idea of loose leash walking and is walking by your side, occasionally stop and ask for a sit. Soon the dog will be walking by your side and sitting when you stop.

Note how Cheryl's leg is slightly bent. She's body blocking my attempt to lean and cross in front of her. She knows body language speaks louder than words to dogs.

A Little Extra Loose Leash Help

 There are tools available to make teaching loose leash walking a little easier. The one that worked best for me is The Gentle Leader, which I am wearing in this picture. There are also other brands. It works on the same principle as a horse harness—guide the head, you guide the animal. It takes a little while for a dog to get used to wearing one, so it's important to take some steps to help the dog adjust to it.

1. Fit the head halter according to the instructions included at time of purchase.

2. Hold the head halter up in front of the dog and show the dog a treat through the nose loop. When the dog reaches her nose through the loop to get the treat, say "Yes" and give the treat. Repeat this a few times.

3. Then put the head halter on the dog and clasp it behind the dog's ears. Give lots of treats. Don't hook the leash on at this point. Just let the dog get used to the feel of something around her nose. If she paws at it, distract her with a treat. Some dogs get very panicked and others just try to slide it off by rubbing their faces. Either way, distract when they mess with the head halter, praise and reward when they leave it alone. Start out leaving the head halter on for short periods of time and then increase the time-frame gradually. Never leave the head halter on all the time or when the dog is alone.

4. Once the dog gets used to the head halter, start hooking the leash on to the loop that hangs below the dog's chin and perform the same steps as above.

5. When your dog begins to learn where to walk happily with you, start to wean her from wearing the head halter. My human carries one in her pocket just in case I start to get too rambunctious. Even well-trained dogs forget what they are supposed to do once in a while.

NOTE: **NEVER** allow the dog to run out to the end of the leash while wearing a head halter. Neck injuries can occur if the dog's head is snapped too briskly. The Gentle Leader is designed to *gently* guide your dog. No harsh snaps are needed. With proper use, a head halter is a safe gentle guide to help your dog learn to walk calmly by your side.

A word about leashes:

Use a nylon, cloth, or leather leash at least 6' long while training. This will allow you enough length to practice skills at a distance like "Come" and "Stay." Loop the leash a few times while working on loose leash walking so the dog doesn't get too far ahead. Don't wrap the leash tightly around your hand. This might cut off circulation and put you in danger if you have a big dog who does decide to take off running. It's better to drop a leash than have your shoulder pulled out of joint.

Flexi-leashes are not the best tool to use while teaching loose leash walking. These leashes continually pull on the dog's collar as they shorten and lengthen. Dogs also key in on the noise of the click when it locks instead of your voice. It's best to stick to a regular leash, but if you insist on using a flexi-leash, at least keep it locked at a length that keeps the dog near your side. The further a dog gets from you the less control you have. Plus people and dogs can trip over unseen flexi-lines crossing their path. Keep your dog with you and under control for both the dog's safety, yours, and the people around you.

 Paws to Ponder

Dogs need consistency, so in order to teach loose leash walking, there should be no walking that includes pulling. If you give in one day and allow pulling, the next day will be that much more challenging. Be patient, be consistent, it will all pay off in the end. If you feel your dog needs to get more exercise, use a long line in a big field and have a release cue that allows your dog to run and explore, i.e. "Go play," "Go sniff." Call the dog back to you before he reaches the end of the leash so there is still no pulling. Use sniffing as a reward to loose leash walking. Treats aren't the only reward in life, so always be on the lookout for real life situations which also reward your dog.

Chapter  9

Catch Me
If You Can

Catch Me If You Can

Ah, there's nothing better than a good game of "Catch-me-if-you-can." Dogs all over the world zealously enjoy this game with their humans. The humans, however, do not seem to have the same fervor for the game. To some dogs there's nothing more exciting than finding a gate or front door open. When the opportunity presents itself, these dogs take off running, occasionally looking back over their shoulder to make sure their human is keeping up. If the person seems to be falling too far behind, the dog will loop around and come in for a closer pass, egging the human to engage in a faster pursuit.

"Come, Fido," a person called to her dog at the park one day. "I told you to COME HERE," she said as she raced after the dog.

When a person plays the "Catch-me-if-you-can" game with a dog, it's almost always a guarantee that the person runs out of steam before the dog. The woman stopped, all stooped over, to catch her breath. The dog also stopped, just out of reach.

"You stupid dog—I said COME." The lady gasped with a scowl on her face.

Now I don't know about you, but when I see a human's face go red as she bares her teeth, the last thing I want to do is go near her. The game of chase is so much more appealing. Dogs are rewarded by things they find fun, so don't engage in a game of "Catch-me-if-you-can" if you truly want your dog to come to you. Instead, if your dog is ignoring your request to come, try sitting down on the ground and engage in a game of "I've-got-something-you-don't." This is another dog favorite.

The premise of this game is if you suddenly stop playing the "Catch-me-if-you-can" game and start playing the "I've-got-something-you-don't" game, your dog will become curious. As you deeply look at something buried in the grass (even if nothing is really there), your dog won't be able to resist and will come over to investigate with you. At this point, you praise your dog for coming to you. I don't care how out-of-breath you are from chasing the dog earlier or how late you are for an appointment, you need to praise and reward the dog for coming to you, or next time the game won't work. Remember, dogs repeat things that are enjoyable. If you catch the dog, scold him, and take him inside to be isolated for a while, he won't want to play the "I've-got-something-you-don't" game again, but he still will love the "Catch-me-if-you-can game." Good luck catching the dog the next time if you follow the "I've-got-something-you-don't" game with a scolding. Keep all games rewarding.

Now the whole point of all this is for the dog who accidentally gets out of the house and refuses to come to her human. There are always going to be times when a dog sneaks out unexpectedly. If you have done your homework, and your dog is well-trained to respond to your request to come, then neither game will be necessary. However, many of my doggie friends are not well-trained at the front door, and tend to run out whenever they get the chance. Is this the dog's fault? All the dog is doing is attempting to explore the vast universe outside his door. The human is the one at fault. Obviously if a dog is dashing out the front door and the human does not want this behavior, the human needs to take the time to teach the dog appropriate behavior instead.

Waiting at the front door is an important behavior for a dog to learn because it could save the dog's life. If a dog darts out the front door and into traffic it could be a tragic ending to the "Catch-me-if-you-can" game. Dogs don't inherently know the dangers of roads, so it is up to humans to keep dogs safe around dangerous situations.

Teaching a dog to wait at the door isn't all that difficult, but like any other training task, it takes time and patience. Learning the "Wait-at-the-door" game can be just as fun as any other game if the human makes it that way. It's important to note that teaching a dog to wait is different than teaching the dog to stay. With "Stay," you want the dog to learn not to move at all. With "Wait," you want the dog to learn to pause and not proceed through something—usually a door or a gate. If the dog wants to walk around in the area he is in, that's all right; the dog just shouldn't pass through the door.

The steps on the next page may be used to teach a dog not to pass through an open house door, a gate, or even a car door. Keep in mind, though, that an unattended open door or gate is an invitation to celebrate the freedom of the great outdoors. These steps usually are more successful when the human is there to remind the dog what is expected.

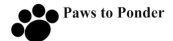 **Paws to Ponder**

Some people say you should never play the "Catch-me-if-you-can" game with a dog. In the right circumstances, with the right training, dogs love to play keep-away. Be sure to first teach your dog to always come to you prior to playing a game where you chase your dog. Then have a cue word that it's all right for the dog to run from you, i.e. "Gonna Getcha."

Always take time to stop the game, call the dog to you, and then praise and reward with more game play. You can have lots of fun with your dog as long as YOU control the game.

Wait

1. Go to the front door. Put your hand on the knob. If your dog lunges towards the door, pull your hand away from the knob.

2. Stand and wait. When your dog backs away, say "Yes" toss a treat toward your dog, and then repeat steps 1 and 2. Only proceed to the next step when the dog no longer responds to your hand on the knob.

3. Turn the knob and start to open the door. If/when the dog lunges toward the door, close it and take your hand off the knob.

4. Stand and wait. When your dog backs away from the door, say "Yes" and toss a treat toward your dog. Repeat steps 3 and 4 until the dog gets the concept.

5. Increase the distance the door opens as the dog improves his waiting skills. Praise and reward any time the dog does not lunge toward the door. Add the verbal cue "Wait" prior to touching the knob.

6. Once your dog masters each stage, move further towards getting out the door. Step back in the house and close the door if the dog starts to follow. Always praise and reward when the dog moves away from the door.

7. Repeat these steps until you can walk out the door without the dog following. Praise and reward any desired behavior at the door.

8. Now you should have a dog who doesn't dart out the door when you open it. Time to start the process all over again with someone on the other side of the door. Adding distractions means starting from step 1. This time the steps should go a little faster, though.

CAUTION:

If necessary, use a leash during this training process to keep your dog safe. Keep the leash tethered to something but be sure it has some slack. The leash is only there to keep the dog from darting out the door and not to hold the dog back during the training. If the leash does all the work, the dog won't learn. Use the leash as a safety tool only.

HINT:

Once your dog has learned to wait at the door, introduce a cue word that means the dog may proceed through the door with you, i.e. "Out." Choose a word that makes sense to you and make sure everyone uses the same word so the dog doesn't become confused. Some people just rely on a leash being hooked on the dog as the "Out" cue. Whatever works best for you as long as everyone in the household is consistent.

Paws to Ponder

All training takes time and patience. Most of us get dogs for the pleasure of their company. That pleasure will increase if you take the time to train your dog to learn proper manners that make both of your lives simpler. Make training a game instead of a chore, so both of you will enjoy the experience.

Chapter **10**

Can You Dig It?

Can You Dig It?

Mother Earth beckoned to me, as did the pesky mole burrowed beneath the dirt. I stuck my nose deep into the grass and took quick sniffs. Wafting up through the layers of soil and sod was the heavenly smell of a mole. Resistance was futile. I had to dig—and dig I did with all my might, following the trail of the mole across the yard. The crafty critter evaded me…this time. Tired after my great hunt, I took a snooze under the forsythia bush where I had dug a cool spot—perfect for a sunny afternoon nap.

I was awoken from a deep slumber by a spine-chilling scream.

"OH NO-ooooo!" My human screamed as he stomped across the yard. "What on earth happened here? My beautiful backyard is filled with trenches. It looks like a war zone." He went on and on. I'm not sure what he was saying, but by the tone of his voice, I decided the safest thing was for me to stay put.

"DELILAH!" He bellowed. I didn't move. "I know you did this. Come out here at once."

Yeah, like that was going to happen. I was sure certain doom was imminent if I went near him at that point. I continued to hide under the bush, crouching down further into my hole for safety.

"I see you over there," he said spying me. Run or stay put was the question coursing through my mind. I decided to give him the big brown sad eyes— that always works with humans. I rolled over on my back and tried to look as sweet and submissive as possible.

"You even dug under there, you b-a-a-a-d dog," he seethed as he reached under and pulled me out from my hiding spot. "Just look what you have done to my yard. You know you aren't supposed to dig."

Truly I didn't know what the problem was—no really, I mean it. I don't have a great command of the English language. What I did get was his voice. He was angry about something, and I didn't want to be the brunt of it. I wasn't capable of making a connection to the digging I did earlier in the yard. Dogs just don't work that way. If he had caught me in the middle of digging and interrupted and redirected my behavior, now that would have meant something to me. After my nap, I couldn't make the connection.

The next day, both my humans were out digging in the yard. Oh boy, I was so excited because these people were enjoying my favorite pastime. I decided to join them. We dug a big square area and then my humans (bless their wonderful little hearts) brought in some more stinky dirt and mixed it in with what we had already churned up. To top it all off, they added toys and biscuits to the mix—my idea of heaven, let me tell you!

Then they put big pieces of wood all around the dirt and declared it a "Digging Box." Wow, if my eyes could get teary with emotion they would! Over the next few days, my humans taught me how to use the "Digging Box." (I wish this was a video instead of a book because you would hear angels sing every time I said "Digging Box!")

My humans must have been dogs in a previous life because they dug with such enthusiasm while teaching me what to do. I soon joined in the digging fun and discovered that if I dug in the box it made my humans happy. For the next two weeks, my humans watched me closely when I was outside and redirected any inappropriate digging to the "Digging Box." I finally figured out that the "Digging Box" was the only place I was allowed to dig. I was happy because I could dig; my humans were happy because their yard wasn't riddled with holes.

My digging box isn't as fancy as some, but
my friends like sharing it with me anyway.
The fancy part is more for you humans. We
dogs just care about digging!

My digging box is located under a tree. This
makes it a nice cool place in the summer. Now,
I dig holes there to sleep in instead of under
the bushes. Success of the digging box is based
on training, location, and keeping the spot
interesting.

Paws to Ponder

Sometimes the best solutions are the ones that meet everyone's needs. It's not just about making the humans happy. Asking a Jack Russell not to dig is like asking a teenager not to text! Jack Russells were designed to dig small vermin out of holes. Don't fight genetics and breeding. Instead allow those urges to happen in an appropriate place.

If you are worried about how a Digging Box will look in your yard, make it part of the landscaping. Use rocks for the border; add mulch to the soil; build a gazebo over top—if you really want to go crazy. Make the Digging Box a beautiful part of your garden and a practical place to redirect your dog's digging. Get creative and have fun!

Chapter **11**

Puppy Love

Puppy Love

Getting a puppy is an exciting time for a family. Puppies are cute and cuddly. Television advertisements and shows portray appealing, well-behaved, adorable pups. What they don't usually reveal, though, is the amount of work that goes into raising a puppy.

For a puppy, getting a new family is both an exciting and scary experience. One minute you are with your mom, brothers, and sisters, and the next minute you are whisked away to a strange place with unfamiliar people. The age of the puppy at this time carries a lot of weight on how well the puppy adjusts to the changes. Some pups are released too early in life. We have fear periods that we go through as pups and most puppies are smack dab in the middle of a fear period at eight weeks old. That's why it's best, if possible, to wait until a puppy is ten to twelve weeks. This not only allows a puppy to experience more from being with his mother and siblings, but allows the pup to get through some fear periods without a lot of trauma.

Never take a puppy prior to eight weeks of age. These pups haven't learned enough from their family and often develop behavioral problems due to their early release from the litter. Of course, there are cases when a puppy is orphaned, and the humans are left to do the best they can in raising and socializing their pup. However, if you have a choice, wait at least until a puppy is eight weeks prior to taking the pup home.

Leaving the comfort of your litter can be a tough time. Here's what life can look like from a puppy's point of view.

My brothers and sisters were great fun. We lived in the country where the air was crisp and clean, and the Blue Ridge Mountains could be seen from our kennel. Life was good. Mom taught us about dog manners like how to settle after dinner and take a nap. My brothers and sisters taught me about proper playing and not biting too hard. If I did bite too hard, they yipped and ignored me. I didn't like that, so I learned a nice soft mouth. I did the same for them if they got too rambunctious.

Every once in a while a nice family would come and look at us. Occasionally they would take one of my brothers or sisters out to play, and then they would take a puppy away. We weren't sad, and we really didn't give it much thought beyond that day. Then one day a man took me. Before I knew what was happening, he put me into a cardboard box inside of what looked like a bigger box. (I now know that it was a car, but I had no clue what it was back then.) As we drove away, I felt my stomach churn. I didn't understand what was happening and was nervous. Suddenly my breakfast was all over the box. I tried to avoid stepping in it, but it was no use. I flattened myself to the bottom of the box and tried not to slide around as we wound our way through curves and over hills.

Finally the big box came to a stop, and I heard the man's voice.

"Got a pup for the kids" he said rather gruffly.

"Ewwww! Oh my gosh. You picked out a dog who gets car sick. Great!" A woman exclaimed as she peered into the box. "I can see where this is going already. You probably expect me to clean the thing up."

"Well, if they hadn't fed her breakfast right before I picked her up, she might have been fine." The man picked up the cardboard box and carried it with me inside. I felt sick all over again as he jostled the box up the front steps. The woman held her breath as she cleaned me in the kitchen sink. Then she put me on the floor, where I instantly peed. After all, it had been a long ride.

"Agggghhhh!" the woman screamed. "She's peeing all over the place."

"She's just a puppy. You shouldn't have put her down without putting her outside first." He seemed like a reasonable man to me.

"I knew if we got a dog, I'd have to think of everything." The woman seemed somewhat upset as she took me outside. I sat in the grass and looked at her. "Well, pee," she said with her hands on her hips. I didn't know what she meant, and looking back on it now, it was a little silly for her to expect me to do something I had just done.

"Ughhh," the woman swooped me up and stomped inside. She set me back down on the floor. Two children came rushing in.

"Look, look, a puppy," they squealed with delight. They scooped me up and spun me around. I felt that breakfast coming back once again. Before you knew it I was being dressed in hats and pushed around in a doll carriage. I was exhausted, but there was no rest for the weary. I wished someone would tell these kids to let me sleep for a while. I was so confused and tired and wanted nothing more than a cozy place to sleep. Fortunately, the children soon grew weary of their games, and put me down on a nice soft carpet. I fell asleep and took a long nap.

When I awoke, no one was around. I whimpered, I cried, and then I pooped and peed. The woman came in and once again screamed. She seemed to do that a lot. I was tossed outside, and there I remained. I grew and grew and grew. I learned that there was a lot of territory to explore, and explore I did. I wandered here and there and was often picked up by very nice people who were kind enough to give me a ride home. Each time I returned, the lady screamed, and the man pointed a finger in my face. They ended up putting me on a chain in the backyard. My wandering days were over. I longed for the days of being dressed up in doll clothes. At least then they paid attention to me.

This, unfortunately, is the fate of many puppies. People don't realize how much work is involved in raising a puppy. Some have never raised a puppy before. Others had a puppy as a child but weren't involved in the day-to-day care. For many, it's been a long time since they've been through the puppy stage, and they've forgotten how much work is required and the sleepless nights involved. Whatever the reason, they expect too much of the pup.

Puppies need to have a quiet safe place to retreat when they first arrive home. A crate is a great place to allow this to happen. The crate should be located in a part of the house where the family hangs out the most so there is no chance of feeling isolated. This also allows the family an opportunity to watch the puppy to see when it's time to take the pup outside. In my case, the family didn't pay enough attention, so I relieved myself in inappropriate places. This was no fault of my own; when nature calls, pups respond. (There's more about crate training and housebreaking in—you guessed it, the

Crate Training and *Housebreaking* chapters.)

Puppies require training the moment they come into your home. Housebreaking routines need to be established and listening skills acquired. Puppies go through development stages just like human children. An "adolescent" phase comes around five to six months when we discover there is a world beyond our family and own yard. During this time we may suddenly appear to no longer listen. At around nine to ten months, we go through a "teenage" stage where we may get an attitude that seems to say, "You can't make me." At one to one-and-half years (sometimes two years), we may come into an "adult" phase where we test to see who is in charge. If you train your puppy from the beginning, these "testing" stages will be much easier to handle. Establish rules from the beginning and constantly enforce them through positive methods. If you do, you will raise a happy, confident

 Paws to Ponder

It takes time and patience to teach a puppy about living in a house. Having a puppy is like having a baby. There may be some sleepless nights in the beginning as the pup learns to adjust to a new home. Don't invite a lot of visitors the first few days after the pup arrives. The puppy is going to require quiet time to adjust, and you will need some time to figure out the new pup's schedule.

Being prepared prior to bringing the pup home will make life much easier. Having a crate, food, bowls, toys, leash, and a collar already at the house will make the transition go more smoothly for both the family and the puppy. If you have not picked out a puppy yet, think twice about the commitment you are about to undertake. The rewards are great, but so is the work and cost. Sometimes an adult dog is a little easier than a puppy, but there is work involved in helping both learn how to live in a human household.

Chapter 12

Adopting an Adult Dog

Adopting an Adult Dog

I was an adult when I came to my current home, and right off the bat my human (who should have known better) made a critical error. When someone came to the door only fifteen minutes after my arrival, she put me in the bedroom. In her defense, she wasn't sure how I would be with visitors, so she was trying to keep everyone safe.

I was only in the bedroom for a few minutes, but I'm guessing by my human's response, it was too long. Being left alone in a new place made me nervous. I jumped up on the big bed and circled around looking for a way to get out. My frustration grew. I started digging at the bed. Before I knew it feathers were flying everywhere.

The reason I had to leave one of my homes is that I had a passion for chickens. The smell of feathers in the comforter really got me going. I dug some more. I dug deep. When my human came into the room, she gasped.

"Oh my gosh. What have you done?" She laughed.

Yes, she actually laughed. I guess I must have looked quite a sight when she opened the door. As you may or may not know, St. Bernards drool when we get nervous or excited. I was drooling as I dug in the bed. Feathers and foam covered my face and body.

"What's the matter?" The man in the house inquired with curiosity.

"Don't come in here. You don't want to know."

I think she was sure he'd say to get rid of me. However, when he entered the room, he too began to laugh. I knew I was in the right place. Seems the man always hated the bed I had destroyed, and now there was an excuse to buy a new one.

I promptly flopped on what was left of the mattress, rolled over and presented a feathery belly, which they both rubbed with delight.

Not every dog is as lucky as I am. Often this kind of scenario will end with the dog being tossed into the backyard. My new humans realized their error—leaving me alone in an unfamiliar place without supervision. They knew punishing me would be pointless.

When choosing a puppy or adult dog, breed is also important to understand. Even if you are adopting a mixed breed from the shelter, a best guess as to what breed possibilities are mixed in the dog can be helpful. Some breeds need a lot of exercise and easily become bored if they are not constantly challenged with exciting activities. Although a little fluffy black and white dog may be cute, this dog could be a Border Collie mix, which is a herding breed. Working dogs have a lot of energy and want a job to do. If you don't find one for them, they may become self-employed and find a job that is not to your liking. A Border Collie is great for an active person who is interested in sports like agility or frisbee to keep the dog busy. However, if you have a quiet home, look for a breed or mix of breeds who tend to be happy lazing around.

Also consider the age of the dog. A puppy may not be the best thing for a quiet laid-back home, but a middle-aged or senior dog might. Doing some research ahead of time and learning as much as you can BEFORE bringing home that cute dog with the sad puppy dog eyes will save you, your family, and the dog a lot of heartache.

 Paws to Ponder

Whether bringing home a puppy or an adult dog, steps can be taken to avoid many problems. All dogs are going to do something wrong in the beginning. It's all part of the process of learning to live in a human world. Even adult dogs may need housebreaking if they have lived outside all their lives, or in a house where they were allowed to eliminate inside. Chewing can be a problem at any age. The following chapters on crate training, housebreaking, and chewing will help you introduce safe concepts to your new furry friend as they learn to fit into your home and family. Don't forget to teach the basic skills mentioned in *The Basics* chapter. Bringing a dog into your family is a lot of work, but the rewards of having a well-behaved canine companion is worth the effort.

Chapter 13

Crate Training

Crate Training

Dogs are den animals. They enjoy having a safe place to go to when they feel uneasy about something or just want to be alone. A crate, when introduced properly, provides a den-like atmosphere for your dog, especially when your dog is young or new to your household. Housebreaking is much easier with a crate as dogs will usually not eliminate in their den. The crate also provides a safe place for destructive dogs to stay when left alone. You can use the crate to keep your dog confined at night or during the day when you are gone. It can also be used for times that you are busy around the house and unable to watch your dog while you are working on housebreaking or have an avid chewer.

It's important to introduce the crate in a positive way so both you and your dog feel this is a good place—not a prison. Plan to have some time at home with your dog to initiate crate training, so you don't have to leave the dog as soon as you bring her home. You can make crate training an enjoyable process for both you and your dog if you take your time with the crate training steps.

It's important to choose the appropriate size crate for your dog. Measure the dog's height to the shoulders and length from chest to base of tail; then add 4 - 6" to each measurement. The dog should be able to comfortably turn around and stand up in the crate.

The crate should never be too large for the size of the dog if you plan to use it as a housebreaking tool. If the crate is too big for the dog, she may sleep in one end and eliminate in the other. A small crate will encourage the dog to wait until taken to a place outside of the den to eliminate, provided the dog is not kept in the crate too long. Many wire crates now come with a divider so you can change the size of the crate as the dog grows.

People wonder whether a wire or plastic crate is better. It's really a matter of preference. Either can be made comfortable for the dog. I prefer a crate where I feel cozy and secure and all closed in. Oliver, my Poodle buddy, likes an open crate where he can see all around. A wire crate can be made cozy with a sheet over it and a bed with bumpers.

Location of the crate is also important. The dog needs to feel a part of the family even when in the crate, so choose a part of the house where everyone spends the most time. It might be advisable to have two crates if you plan on having the dog in the bedroom. That way the dog can sleep in the same room with you and feel more secure by being with other "pack" members.

Delilah's Rules to Remember for Crate Training

RULE #1:

A dog should never be kept in a crate longer than six to eight hours. We get bored. If your dog needs to be confined to a crate for eight hours, hire a dog sitter to come mid-day to play and walk your dog. Otherwise, you may have a very hyper misbehaving dog when you come home.

RULE #2:

Puppies should be kept in a crate only as long as the number of hours that they are months in age, i.e. a four-month old puppy should not be in a crate longer than four hours, and no puppy should be kept crated longer than five hours. Not only are puppies unable to hold their bladders for long periods, behavior problems from boredom and lack of socialization may occur if puppies are isolated too long. It would be considered neglect to keep a human child in a playpen for hours on end. Although puppies are not humans, they have a need to be with their humans in order to grow mentally and physically and to learn how to be a good canine citizen.

Crate Training Steps

Crate

Note:

Don't push your dog through these steps too quickly. Some dogs have confinement issues and need to learn the crate is a safe place. If this is the case, the dog may need some extra time to adjust to being left in a crate. If your dog makes frantic attempts to get out of the crate despite following these steps, then you may have a dog who is suffering from separation anxiety or confinement issues. Proceed through the steps slowly. Professional assistance may be necessary if your dog causes injury to himself trying to escape from the crate even after going through all these steps.

1. Toss treats in the crate and allow the dog to go in and out freely. DO NOT FORCE YOUR DOG INTO THE CRATE! The dog needs to learn that going in and out of the crate is no big deal.

2. If your dog refuses to go in the crate, try using more enticing treats. You can also feed your dog near the crate and slowly start to move the food dish into the crate. Your dog will begin to get hungry and want to enter the crate to eat.

3. DO NOT close your dog into the crate in the beginning. Allow your dog to feel comfortable with the idea of going in and out of the crate first. Use a bungee cord to hold the door open, so it doesn't accidentally close and scare the dog.

4. Once your dog is comfortable with the crate, begin to close the door for short periods of time. Just a minute at first, then increase the time. Give the dog lots of praise and a treat when you open the door.

5. As you increase the time the dog is in the crate with the door closed, stay in sight at first. Ignore whining and barking. If you let your dog out when she's whining or barking, your dog will only start whining and barking more when put in the crate.

Don't stop here!
There are more steps to achieve on the next page.

Cont.

6. When your dog is comfortable with the crate while you are in the room, start to go out of sight for short periods of time and slowly increase the time that you are in another room.

7. Once your dog is comfortable in the crate with you out of the room, work up to leaving the house. Again, start with short periods and slowly increase the time you are gone. Leave your dog with a special, safe toy for entertainment.

8. After a while your dog will learn that being in the crate is just fine.

9. Never put your dog in the crate in an angry way. If you need to use the crate as a time out for an overactive or misbehaving dog, be sure to use a calm voice and tell your dog "Quiet time" as you give him a safe toy in the crate. Leave the dog in the crate only for a short time and then allow him to come out and practice calmer behavior.

12. A dog should never be kept in a crate longer than six to eight hours. If your dog needs to be confined to a crate for eight hours, hire a dog sitter to come mid-day to put your dog out and spend some time playing with your dog. Otherwise, you may have a very hyper misbehaving dog when you come home.

Happy Crate Training!

HINT:

Give your dog a food toy such as the KONG (a rubber toy) stuffed with goodies. Make this toy something she gets only when she's in the crate. (See *Helping the Chew-a-holic* chapter for more information on KONG toys.) When she starts to associate the crate with yummy treats she doesn't get elsewhere, she'll jump for joy at the idea of going in the crate.

Chapter **14**

Housebreaking Rules: Pups and Adults

 Paws to Ponder

This chapter is about housebreaking not housetraining. If you want your dog to eliminate outside, start teaching your dog to go outside from the first day you bring your dog home no matter what the dog's age. Don't use newspaper or pee pads inside. This teaches your dog that eliminating inside is all right. Later you will have to undo this habit and retrain the dog to go outside. Start with the desired behavior to avoid confusing the dog and causing yourself a lot of frustration. The housebreaking process will go so much smoother for both you and dog.

Housebreaking Rules for Pups and Adult Dogs

Housebreaking should start as soon as you arrive home with your new dog, whether a puppy or an adult. Many people mistakenly think that adult dogs are already housebroken. Adult dogs may be quicker at picking up on the rules than a puppy, but they still need to be trained. Although I was housebroken in my last home, I still needed to learn which door to go to, what signals to give, and where I was supposed to relieve myself in my new home.

In order to avoid having accidents right from the beginning, take the dog to the area you designate as the potty spot (make sure it's not too far from the house), BEFORE you even bring the dog inside for the first time. Let the dog explore around. (You may want to keep a leash on the dog, even inside a fenced yard, so he'll stay in the potty spot.) If the dog goes potty, praise and give a small treat. If the dog doesn't go, don't worry. Some dogs, especially adult shelter dogs, may not relieve themselves for days after being adopted. Just be sure to watch the dog closely when inside and take the dog to the potty spot frequently. They can't hold it forever.

People's houses are big places to a dog, and sometimes a back bedroom seems like it's far away from what the dog considers "the den." Most dogs will not go in their den, unless they have been given no other choice. However, a huge house does not seem like one entire den to a dog. We figure if the family hangs out in one room most of the time, the rest of the rooms are not part of the den. Start by keeping the dog in a smaller area of the house until housebreaking concepts are totally understood.

How does a human decide if the dog understands housebreaking? Is the dog having frequent accidents in the house? If so, the dog doesn't get it. It's that simple. We don't pee on the rug to get humans angry. We pee because we have to or because we are stressed or ill. If a dog is peeing on the rug after years of being housebroken, that is the time for a veterinarian visit, not necessarily housebreaking.

Go Potty

1. Take your dog out to the spot you want him to potty when you first bring him home. Praise your dog if he pees or poops.

2. When you take your dog inside after peeing or pooping, set your watch, alarm clock, or a timer to ring in two hours (longer for adult dogs). When the alarm goes off, take your dog outside to the potty spot and say "Go potty" or whatever cue you would like to use (the key is to be consistent). Give the dog about five minutes or so to go. Praise and give a small treat for any pees or poops. If the dog does not go, take him back inside and try again in ten minutes. During this ten minutes, watch the dog closely or put him in his crate. This is often the time for an accident to happen.

3. Once the dog goes potty outside and has been rewarded with treats, playtime, and maybe a walk, go back inside and set your alarm for another two hours. Soon you will work out your dog's rhythm and know how frequently your dog needs to go outside.

4. Dogs need consistency. Always take your dog out as soon as he wakes up, after he eats or drinks, and when he has been chewing on a toy or playing for awhile. Have the dog walk to the door with you so he will learn the pattern of going to the door when he needs to go out. Watch for signs which may indicate that the dog needs to go potty.

Housebreaking Steps

Here are some steps to make housebreaking a fast (about one - two weeks depending on the age of the dog) and a fairly easy process provided you don't skip any steps or rush through them. You will need to have some time to work on this, so if you work outside of the home, now is the time to use some of those vacation hours you have saved up.

Body language that indicates a pooch needs to be taken out:

Pacing

Panting

Circling

Sniffing

Whining

Potty Teaching Tools

CRATES: A crate is a very helpful tool in housebreaking. (Be sure to read the Chapter on *Crate Training* to learn more about this process.) Dogs usually have the natural tendency not to go potty in their sleeping area unless they have been crated too long and have no other choice. Once the dog is allowed to soil in the crate, your job of housebreaking will be more difficult, so be sure not to leave the dog in a crate for more than a few hours in the beginning.

BELL: Put the crate by your bed at night and attach a bell inside the crate where the puppy will bump it. This way you will hear when the puppy is getting restless. You can also hang a bell on the door used to go outside to the potty spot. Put a little peanut butter on it to get the dog to touch it in the beginning. When the dog touches the bell with his nose, and it rings, praise the dog, and open the door to go out. Each time encourage the dog to ring the bell. The door opening becomes the reward. If you are dealing with a young pup, hold off on teaching the bell until the puppy is older, or you may end up with a puddle by the back door while the pooch waits for you to answer.

ALARM: If you are a sound sleeper or one who loses track of time during the day, an alarm is a great tool to keep you and the puppy on schedule during the housebreaking process. Establishing a routine is up to you. Dogs have a natural rhythm that you will learn, but they don't know how to tell you they need to go in the beginning. Set an alarm for every one to two hours during the day and no longer than five hours at night. Once you work out your dog's pattern, you can revise how often you reset the alarm.

DOG SITTER: A puppy's system needs to mature before being able to go for longer periods of time between eliminating. Adult dogs may stress if left alone for hours on end. Hiring a dog sitter to come during the day if you are gone long hours can help. Advise the dog sitter to take time to play with your dog after she has been taken out of the crate and gone potty. If the dog is put immediately back in the crate, she may begin to realize that if she holds off peeing and pooping, she can stay out of the crate longer.

PATIENCE: Housebreaking takes time and patience. If you have not yet picked out a dog, give a lot of consideration to your choice of adding a canine companion. We are great to have around, but we are a big responsibility.

 Paws to Ponder

Make sure to clean up any accidents completely. If the accident is on a rug, cleaning all the way to the pad underneath is necessary to get rid of the smell. Blot the area as dry as possible and clean with a deodorizing cleanser. Some special cleansers are made which contain enzymes to remove urine odor. Do not use ammonia as it will smell like urine to your dog and cause her to return to the same spot.

Accidents in the house are almost unavoidable in the beginning unless you are extremely diligent. It is important that you do not punish your dog in any way when accidents happen. The dog will only associate the punishment with the act instead of the location and be fearful of going potty in your presence. Instead, when you catch your dog in the act, gently interrupt her with an "Oops," and take her outside. When she relieves herself outside, praise her. Rubbing her nose in an accident or hitting her with newspaper after the fact will only confuse the dog and not help in the housebreaking process at all. The only time you should use a rolled up newspaper when there is an accident is to smack yourself on the back of your hand and say, "Bad, bad person for not watching the dog closer."

Chapter  15

Helping
the
Chew-a-holic

Helping the Chew-a-holic

Some dogs seem addicted to chewing. In their minds, everything in the house is a chew toy. A young dog needs to chew to help teeth break through the gums. Older dogs need to chew to exercise their jaws, and well, chewing is just plain fun! Unfortunately, there isn't much you can do to stop your dog's natural need and desire to chew.

There are some products that can be purchased to make items taste yucky, i.e. Bitter Apple, Bitter Yuck. Some of my doggie friends find them very tasty and seem pleased with the added flavor. Personally, I don't like them, so I stay away from anything sprayed with them. If your dog is one of those who likes the flavor, there is still hope. You can redirect a dog's chewing to appropriate items. When your dog begins to chew something inappropriate, offer to trade an appropriate toy with the item he currently has. He'll happily trade once he learns he will get something great in return, and you will be able to save many shoes (and other items) from destruction. The following are some suggestions for great, safe toys and games for the avid chewer.

Meet the KONG

A KONG is a hard rubber toy shaped like a honeycomb. You can stuff yummy treats inside to keep the dog chewing and playing longer. There are a variety of sizes and strengths: pink and blue ones for pups, red for medium chewers, black for tough chewers, and purple for seniors. They are virtually indestructible, but there are dogs out there who can chew up anything, so always watch your dog with toys to make sure the dog is safe.

Making the KONG Wonderful

After my bed eating episode (see the chapter entitled *Adopting an Adult Dog* if you are skipping around and missed the story), my human quickly worked to turn me into a KONG-A-HOLIC. Using quality canned dog food and some kibble, part of my daily meals were fed to me in my KONG. At first my human stuffed it loosely so I could learn how to toss it around and get the food out. After I became a pro, she stuffed the KONG more firmly and even froze it. She used a variety of food—peanut butter, cheese, baby food turkey, canned dog food, and kibble. YUM! I couldn't wait to find out what was layered in my wonderful KONG each day. This was much better than chewing up feather comforters and foam beds!

Be sure to clean the KONG frequently. My human puts it on the top rack of the dishwasher. I don't know if you are supposed to do that, but it seems to work for her. I don't leave a whole lot of food in it, but I heard complaints about all the slobber. What's the big deal?

Games with the KONG

Games can also be played with the KONG. One time my human put a rope through the hole at the end of the KONG, stuffed it, then hung it from a branch on a tree. I had to move around and try to get it to hold still to get the goodies out. I guess it was kind of like a doggie form of a piñata! I got worn out jumping and running around. Eventually it was taken out of the tree, and I was allowed to finish emptying it in the shade.

Another fun game is playing "Treasure Hunt" with the KONG. When my human is going to be gone for the day, she hides KONGS around the house for me to find. This keeps me busy and out of trouble. At first she had to show me how to find hidden treats and KONGS by pointing out hiding places, but now I'm a pro at sniffing them out on my own. Be careful using this game, though, if you have multiple dogs. Some dogs don't like to share food and high value treats, so this game is often best played in a single dog home.

DELILAH'S HINT:

I have several KONGS so my human doesn't have to worry if there is a clean one available. She stuffs a bunch on the weekend and then puts them in the freezer where they are quickly available. I wish I had opposable thumbs so I could get into that freezer. Oh well, that's why having a human is so great.

Other Toy Options

There are other durable toys on the market. Original *Nylabones* are hard plastic bones that many dogs enjoy chewing, especially those who have an affinity for plastic (i.e. the ones who choose Barbies and Legos as chew toys).

Buster Cubes are a great form of entertainment. These cubes can be filled with dry kibble. As the dog pushes the cube around, kibble slowly falls out rewarding the dog as he plays. As with the KONG, some dogs need a little help figuring out this toy at first.

The *Tug-A-Jug* can be another fun food toy. Sometimes it's more work than I like, so I wait for my friends Oliver or Jasper to knock it around, and I follow to pick up the food. Always be careful when using food toys in multiple dog households. Not all dogs share as nicely as we do.

The *Twist-a-Treat* is a soft rubber toy that holds food. It's like the KONG and can be tossed around until the treats fall out.

These days there are a lot of food and interactive toys on the market, so give a few a try and find out what your dog likes.

Paws to Ponder

Many people will turn to rawhide bones to help satisfy a dog's chewing needs. However, with some dogs, they disappear quickly. Too much rawhide, especially in big pieces, is often hard for a dog to digest and may get clogged inside their intestines. If a dog chews off and swallows big chunks of a rawhide bone, it is better to find an alternative toy. Beef marrow bones are enjoyable chew toys for dogs.

Safety is always important when dogs are playing with toys. Watch your dog with any new toy to make sure it will be safe. Every dog is different. Some will just carry stuffed toys around and never tear them apart; others will rip the same toy to shreds in seconds. Always check labels on toys you purchase for your dog. Be sure if you are purchasing a toy designed for fetching, that you don't leave that toy with your dog to chew. Chances are it was designed for interactive play with a human and will not hold up to rigorous chewing. Inspect your dog's teeth to make sure hard toys and bones are not wearing them down. Throw away worn toys, even if it is the dog's favorite one. A shabby toy can be a dangerous one that may cause intestinal blockage or choking.

Chapter **16**

A
Bit
About
Bites

A Bit about Bites

Dogs have teeth—well most of them. Dental care is important for dogs. Humans should brush their dog's teeth regularly to prevent tooth decay. Ah, but I digress. As I was saying…

Dogs have teeth. We use them to chew. We use them to hold things. We use them to play. We use them to give warnings. We also may use them to bite—either to protect, to warn, or to capture prey. In the dog world, using teeth isn't frowned upon as much as it is in the human world. We communicate many messages with our teeth. Baring our teeth says, "Back off. I'm not comfortable with what's happening." An air snap means, "You are way too close." Holding another dog down with teeth around the dog's neck means, "You've really overstepped your bounds. Say 'uncle,' and I'll release you." When done properly, communication with teeth shouldn't leave a single mark. It's all part of our body language used to communicate our desires to others.

Occasionally dogs do fight leaving puncture wounds and scratches on one or both dogs. This occurs when dogs involved in the fight refuse to back down or the arousal level is too high for the dogs to stop. Fortunately, these types of fights are rare. Training dogs to look away from offending dogs can help defuse fights of this caliber. (See *The Basics* chapter to learn how to teach "Leave it.")

Dog-to-dog fights in multiple dog households are usually over resources—food, bones, toys, or even certain people. Once you recognize the triggers, it's best to remove them. Many times the other dogs realize that the leader dog should not be challenged for these items. If it's a young dog trying to assert himself, a quick stare, growl, or air snap from the leader is normally enough to put the youngster in his place. When there are two dogs of the same age, there can be more controversies as they try to find their place in the pack. Dogs will often live in harmony through the first year of life and then surprise their humans by getting into fights at one-and-a-half to two years of age. This is most likely due to the dog maturing and trying out new behaviors to see the results. If they get away with it, the behaviors may continue.

Most dogs prefer to be led rather than lead. Being the leader is a lot of work. You have to watch the other dogs and make sure they are following the rules. Even if you are enjoying sunning yourself on a lazy spring day, the leader has to get up to intervene if a skirmish is about to occur. It's a tough job. When my human is in the yard, she is the leader and controls all the activities, and that's just fine by me. Only if she requests my help do I step in. However, neither of us leads with force. She doesn't ever strike us with anything, and I don't bite hard with my teeth to make a point to another dog, and I never use teeth on humans.

People enjoy the company of their dogs, but when teeth come in contact with human skin, it's upsetting to the human. Dogs learn at a young age how to bite appropriately from playing with their mother and litter mates. Yes, I said appropriately. In the dog world we don't learn not to bite our pack members; we learn HOW to bite properly. During play as a pup, we learn how hard we can bite in order for the game to continue. If we bite too hard, our siblings stop playing and walk away. Since playing is fun, we learn to modify our bite intensity so as not to cause our siblings to ignore us.

Unfortunately, humans don't always realize the importance of the time spent with our doggie families. Many puppies are taken away too young and miss out on valuable life lessons from mom and siblings. Then it is up to the humans to teach proper use of teeth; this is a lot harder for a human to teach than another dog. That's one reason why puppies should not be taken away from their litter mates until at least eight weeks old, but I think it's even better to wait until puppies are ten to twelve weeks old. This gives them plenty of time to learn from their siblings, to get past fear periods, and become better-adapted pups. Puppies put into a human family prior to eight weeks often have more trouble with biting because they have never learned to properly use their mouths.

Does that mean pups received after eight weeks won't have mouthing problems? Nope! Dogs don't have hands, so we use our mouths to explore and play. Puppies are also teething, so they really have a need to chew and mouth. When a puppy is brought into the home, people need to take the time to teach a young pup how to have a soft mouth with humans. Human skin is a lot more sensitive than a furry dog, so puppies need to learn first how soft their mouths need to be with humans and then not to put mouths on humans at all.

Now, you are probably wondering why on earth I'm saying that dogs need to learn how to have a soft mouth with humans if they are going to eventually be taught not to have mouths on humans at all. There may be a time when a dog is startled and then turns to snap. If the dog has been conditioned to have a soft mouth on humans, the tooth/skin contact is much more likely to be soft or better yet, non-existent.

I remember the day little Katie, a Cocker/Shih Tzu mix, got her tail stuck in a door. It hurt a lot, and she turned to snap at the ankle of the person closing the door. She didn't bite down, but it got the attention of the human who then realized what had happened and opened the door. Poor little Katie still has a kink in her tail from this episode. Had she actually bitten down, it wouldn't really be her fault, but any bite in the human world has the potential to be a death sentence for a dog. Since Katie learned how to use a soft mouth as a puppy, no marks were left when she warned her human.

It's crucial to take the time to teach puppies when they are young about bite inhibition. Once they reach adulthood, it may be too late. Dog bite laws are getting stricter as more dogs are living in our communities. Teaching your dog to be a confident, well-adjusted dog in society is of upmost importance. Don't wait until there is a problem. Start training the minute your dog comes into your home. If you realize your dog has a problem accepting other dogs or people, get professional help to teach your dog to overcome these fears, thereby decreasing the chance of a nasty bite incident with sometimes very negative consequences. Taking positive steps in the beginning will help you and your dog have a positive and long-lasting relationship with each other and the community in which you live.

NOTE:

These steps should be practiced with a puppy four-months-old or younger. Adult jaws are formed around five months making these steps dangerous to perform on most dogs. Since puppies need to learn that they should never bite children, only adults should do this training.

Puppy Biting Part I

1. Allow the puppy to mouth and play-bite your hands. Say a high-pitched quick "OUCH!" when the puppy puts slightly more pressure than usual. This sound is meant to interrupt the puppy play momentarily.

2. Immediately stop playing. Cross your arms and turn your back if the dog is still trying to bite.

3. Then allow him to mouth and play again when the pup is calmer.

4. Repeat the "Ouch!" and stop playing every time the puppy applies too much pressure. Do not make this sound too excited or it will rev up the pup. Just one quick sound will do.

5. If the puppy is not responding to the "Ouch," just stop playing and get up and move away for a minute, then start again.

6. The puppy will quickly learn that the fun ends when he mouths too hard.

7. Practice several times a day for 3-4 weeks before proceeding to Part II.

REMEMBER: ONLY ADULTS SHOULD DO THIS TRAINING AND ONLY WITH YOUNG PUPPIES.

Puppy Biting Part II

1. This time *every* time the puppy's teeth make contact with human skin, say "OUCH!"

2. Immediately stop playing and get up and leave.

3. Ignore the puppy for a minute or two.

4. Soon the puppy will start to believe that humans are very sensitive and any tooth contact is a no-no.

5. Remember that puppies do need to mouth and explore, so be sure to provide them with plenty of ways to safely teethe and chew. Safe chew toys, such as a KONG stuffed with goodies, help satisfy your dog's need to chew. Redirect any inappropriate chewing or mouthing to appropriate toys. (See the chapter entitled *Helping the Chew-a-holic* for more information about safe chew toys.)

6. Avoid loose pants, flowing skirts, and loose shoe laces that will entice a dog to chase and bite. Teach children not to run around the puppy. Join a puppy playgroup so that the puppy can learn from other puppies how to play appropriately. (Make sure your puppy is up-to-date on all possible shots before entering a puppy class.)

Have fun with your pup while you teach her the no-bite game!

Puppy Biting Part II:

The puppy should now understand what a soft mouth means—a crucial skill. All dogs may bite at some point if stressed or hurt, so it's important they know how to bite softly.

Now it's time to teach him not to mouth people at all with Part II of the training.

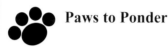 **Paws to Ponder**

These steps are to be performed with young puppies not adult dogs. Once a dog reaches six months, they have powerful adult jaws. If you have an adult dog who bites, seek professional help immediately. An uncontrolled biting dog is a major liability.

Most aggression is fear-based. Working on eliminating the fear can help eliminate aggression tendencies. Some aggression cannot be overcome 100%, but steps can be taken to change some behaviors and manage others. Do not wait thinking the dog will eventually stop biting. Usually these problems become worse if ignored. Get help immediately.

Rough-housing with dogs encourages mouthing and should be avoided. If someone in the household is insistent on rough-housing, there should be rules to go with the game. Have a cue word that means the game begins and one to end the game. Start and stop the game throughout play using the cue words. The person should always be in control of any game and be able to stop the game and have the dog instantly settle. If the dog cannot settle each time the cue for "Game over" is said, then the game should not be played. Children should never rough-house with dogs.

Chapter **17**

Dogs Bark,
Birds Sing,
and
People Talk

Dogs Bark, Birds Sing, and People Talk

Dogs bark (with the exception of the Basenjis who have a great yodel instead). We bark when we are happy. We bark when we greet others. We bark when we play. We bark to warn. We bark when we're bored. It's all perfectly normal dog behavior. Birds sing—it's normal bird behavior. People encourage birds to come to their window with bribes of bird seed so they can hear what birds do naturally—sing. Yet when dogs do what they do naturally—bark, we are admonished. It's not fair!

People talk. It's a normal behavior. While growing up, humans are encouraged to engage in conversation and are taught that it is not nice to interrupt. (Well, most are taught this. I think I've met a few humans who weren't properly trained.) People learn when to talk, when not to talk, or when to whisper.

I'm confused, then, as to why humans don't find it logical to teach dogs when it is or is not appropriate to bark. I know what an "inside voice" is so I can whisper at appropriate times. I also know to stop barking when my human asks me too. How do I know these things? My human taught me. She doesn't forbid me to bark, instead we have come up with cues on when it is appropriate or not. Most people would just be happy to find the off switch on their dog's barking, but often that doesn't allow a dog to do what comes naturally—bark.

One of the roles dogs have long played in the human world is to warn of any impending dangers or intruders. The problem is most of the time dogs don't know how to distinguish between an intruder and someone who is supposed to be there. Every day when my neighbor went to get her mail, I felt it was my duty to announce to my household that someone was approaching. My human, on the other hand, felt this wasn't necessary. However, for me, it seemed like an important duty, so we had to find a compromise. I was taught that barking was all right when there was someone there, but as soon as my human said "Enough," I had to stop. This made sense to me. I was barking to announce an intruder. My human, the leader in our family, would tell me she was aware of the situation and would take it from there with a quick "Enough." She also adds a "Thank you" in the beginning to be polite, but some people laugh at her for doing it. I think it's nice, because the "Thank you" seems to help keep her voice more pleasant. If she doesn't use "Thank you" and barks out "Enough" then I know I've overstepped my bounds.

There may be other situations where you want to teach your dog that barking is not appropriate at all. When we are out walking on a leash, barking is not allowed (unless my human gives me a cue to bark). If I am unsure of a situation while on a leash, I look to my human for guidance. I was taught to do this with a "Look" cue. (Review *The Basics* chapter if you don't know how to teach this cue.)

The following steps are designed to help you teach your dog how to stop

Turning on the bark:

barking when alerting you of some potential threat. If your dog is barking due to boredom, these steps will not help. Your dog is trying to entertain himself, and you will need to solve his boredom problem before you can turn off the barking problem.

Read all instructions BEFORE starting. Including the ones on the next page.

Finding the "on" switch for barking is usually not difficult as most people know what makes their dog bark.

1. Ring the doorbell (or whatever other stimulus causes your dog to bark).

2. Once the dog is barking proceed to the next section.

(See this is why you were supposed to read all the instructions first. If you didn't, you are now trying to see what to do next while your dog is giving you a headache barking. Training humans can be so hard sometimes!)

More steps on the next page.

Note:

Start by teaching the dog while on a leash and close by for better control. Then increase the distance as the dog becomes better at becoming quiet.

Turning off the bark:

Once the dog starts barking, it's time to teach the dog how to turn it off.

1. When the dog starts barking, put a very tasty treat in front of the dog's nose and let the dog sniff it.

2. Say "Quiet" or "Enough" as the dog sniffs the food. The dog cannot sniff and bark at the same time.

3. After a moment of quiet, give the dog the food. Don't give the treat the instant the dog stops barking or you will reward the bark.

4. Repeat the above steps several times over several days or weeks.

5. If food is not enough to get the dog to stop barking, try interrupting the bark by clapping your hands or making another loud sound. Make sure the sound only interrupts the bark and doesn't send the dog running in fear. Reward for quiet behavior.

Keep reading for more steps on using this in real-life situations.

Using the off switch in real life—Once the dog has an off switch for barking, set up situations that are typically a problem, i.e. people or dogs passing the house.

Inside voice:

I was taught an inside voice through capturing my whisper bark. Every time I did a quiet bark, my human rewarded me. Eventually she added the cue word "whisper." This allows me to bark quietly on cue. We really only use it as a trick. When I'm excited I usually bark loud, so my human then uses the "Enough" cue.

1. Wait for the dog to begin barking.

2. After three barks, say "Thank you" just once (it's the polite thing to do to tell us we've done a good job) and then follow it with a pleasant and confident "Quiet" or "Enough." Pick a word and stick with it.

3. Show treats in front of the dog. Reward after a few seconds of quiet. High quality treats may be necessary depending on the level of distractions. Fade the food from training when the dog starts to get the concept. (See the *Will Work for Food* chapter on how to do this properly.)

4. If the dog is quiet on her own, be sure to praise and reward the dog. After all, this is the behavior you want. The idea is to teach the dog that being quiet brings a reward, not the actual barking.

Most of the time people are interested in teaching their dog to stop barking when far away in the backyard. You have to gradually build up to teaching this. Dogs don't generalize very well, and although we may learn to be quiet when you are standing right next to us, we may not get it right away at a distance.

Once you are getting reliable quiets from your dog while you are close by, use a long leash and start increasing the distance. Let your dog go a short distance away at first. Tell the dog, "Thank you, that's enough," when the dog starts barking, and show the dog the treat. If the dog is not looking, call the dog's name with an excited voice and start to run backwards away from the dog. The sound of your voice and the motion will hopefully be enough to distract the dog and get him to look at you (or use the "Look" cue from *The Basics* chapter if it has been taught reliably). Continue to call the dog and reward as soon as the dog gets to you. Usually the dog is no longer barking while he is running to you. A squeaky toy is another way to get a dog to look away from distractions and at you.

It helps to have your dog know a reliable "Come" cue. (See the chapter on *The Basics* for instructions on how to teach this skill.) Then gradually build to adding more distractions and distance. Make sure to have some really good rewards ready so your dog will want to leave whatever he is barking at and come to you. It's hard to be cooler than a squirrel, so you have to increase the benefits when there are tough distractions dogs would rather bark at and chase.

For a rambunctious dog, you will have to be very patient with the process. Start with minor distractions that stimulate the dog to bark and make sure they are a distance away from the dog in the beginning so as not to be too overwhelming. Close the distance and eventually add more distractions in training as the dog learns. Baby steps are necessary with some dogs. Be patient, some of us don't catch on as quickly as others.

For dogs who bark while you are gone, consider the following:

1. Never leave the dog outside while you are gone. Too many things can stimulate barking.

2. Be sure to leave the dog confined in an area of the house that will not allow the dog access to see outside. Leave plenty of stimulating toys for the dog to play with—a KONG or a Buster Cube. Hide toys like stuffed KONGS around the house for your dog to seek and find. (See the Chapter entitled *Helping the Chew-o-holic* for more information on toys to entertain your dog.)

3. Be sure not to leave your dog alone for too many hours a day. Find a dog sitter if necessary. A bored dog is a barking dog.

 Paws to Ponder

There are times when you may or may not want your dog to bark. If you know your dog barks at inappropriate times, teaching alternative behaviors during those times will help your dog learn better behaviors. For instance, if you are approaching another person and your dog often barks, use the steps in the chapter on fear to help your dog accept other people. If your dog barks at other dogs when you are out walking, follow the steps in the chapter entitled *Meeting and Greeting Other Dogs*. Don't get angry at your dog for doing what dogs do naturally, just help your dog learn another behavior or to stop the barking when you ask.

Chapter 18

Things that Go Bump: Helping the Fearful Dog

Things that go Bump!—Helping the Fearful Dog

Fear—it actually can be good at times. Being fearful is the body's way of reacting when there is danger. Fear keeps people from walking down a scary dark alley or going into some other type of dangerous situation. Many dogs have fears too. Some are rational; some are not. One time there was a big loud bang in my neighbor's yard. The humans seemed to enjoy the bang, but I sure didn't. Every instinct in my body told me that a big bang like that was a bad thing and to get out of there fast. I couldn't understand that the bang was something man-made and under control. I just knew that a big loud sound happened in my neighbor's yard, so that was a place to stay away from. Now this might be a good thing if a dog has a habit of wandering over to the neighbor's house uninvited, but our neighbors wanted me to visit with my human. However, after that bang, I wanted nothing to do with going over there.

It took only one night with a loud bang to scare me, and quite a few months to help me overcome my fear of the yard. You see, dogs don't always make the right connections when it comes to fear. If they are scared by something in a certain location, that location, or an item near that location, becomes a trigger for fear.

Here's another example of how an item can become a trigger. A Golden Retriever I know named Goldie…yeah, I know, some humans are not very original…anyway…Goldie was walking with her human down the street when a big dog came rushing out of his house and jumped on her. Nearby was a big trash collection bin. From that point on, whenever Goldie saw a big trash bin, she began to look nervously around and refused to go any further. She mistakenly figured that the big trash bin was an indicator of danger and became fearful of all big trash bins not just the area where the attack happened.

People may think dogs are a little silly by making these connections, but in our minds we are protecting ourselves from what seems like an indication of danger. If we feel that avoiding big trash bins means not being attacked, then isn't it wise to stay away from them? It all makes perfect sense to us. To humans, though, it becomes an annoyance. The human wants to walk down the street, and the dog stops and refuses to pass a big trash bin on the road—a major obstacle to walking a dog on garbage day! So what is a human to do when a dog develops erroneous fears?

Discovering the trigger of the fear is immensely helpful. My human was smart and figured out pretty quick what the trigger was with me and my neighbor's yard. Sometimes it's obvious, and sometimes the human has to do a little more detective work. One of my lab friends named Bud suddenly developed a fear of the kitchen. The humans thought maybe a pan had been dropped while preparing a meal or that Bud had been stepped on during the hustle and bustle of kids running around. When working on those problems didn't solve the kitchen fear, the humans were baffled.

I was brought onto the scene to see if I could lead Bud into the kitchen and demonstrate there wasn't anything to fear. The problem was instantly apparent to me. As soon as I walked into the kitchen, I looked up at the kitchen light. It was buzzing. The buzzing was irritating to the dog's ears, so Bud started to avoid the kitchen. Even during the day when the light was not on, the dog avoided that area. He didn't know it was the light, he just knew there was a sound he didn't like in the kitchen. As soon as I looked at the light, my human tuned into the buzzing sound and the light was fixed. Just a few play sessions with me in the kitchen solved his fear after that.

Sometimes a fear can develop from the smallest of things—a new clock ticking on the bedside table, a wind chime added to the garden outside the window, or as in Bud's case, a buzzing light. People really have to become a pet detective and investigate every new addition to the house when a sudden seemingly unexplainable fear crops up in their dog. Once the problem is found and fixed, if you don't have a St. Bernard around to help out (most people don't, at least not a special one like me), try playing a favorite game or slowly feeding the dog closer and closer to the feared area or object. That way he can see for himself there is no longer anything to worry about.

With my fear of my neighbor's yard, my human worked with me gradually to build my confidence. Since I'm not really food motivated when I'm scared, she couldn't entice me into the neighbor's yard with goodies. Instead, she got a lawn chair, walked to the edge of the property with me on a leash and sat down on the chair. She didn't say anything—didn't ask me to do anything—just sat and started reading a book. This intrigued me. I had no idea what was going on. Eventually I got bored, so I sat down calmly at her side. She stroked my fur and told me I was a good dog. I LOVE to hear that, so I promptly rolled over to get a belly rub. Ah, now that's what life is all about!

Then she stood up, picked up her chair, and moved a few steps closer to my neighbor's yard. I got suspicious and hesitated at the edge and safety of our own yard. I was on a long leash, but I couldn't go back into my yard any further than I was. I sat there for a while watching her read her book. Since I'm not one to enjoy sitting by myself, I slowly crept closer to her and sat down at her side. Again she praised me, rubbed my back, and then my belly, which I happily presented. After a few minutes, she picked up her chair, and we went home. That was it. That was all we did. Curious.

At the time, I had no idea what my human was up to. Every few days we went to the outskirts of my neighbor's yard and did the same thing, slowly creeping more and more into the yard, only inches at a time. My human is so smart! She knew that if she went further than that I would freeze and not move. By doing it in very small steps, I wasn't really aware of what was going on. Through a slow desensitization process, I saw that the yard was not such a scary place and slowly got used to going further and further into it. After a while, I forgot about my fears, and no longer minded going to visit my neighbor (when invited, of course—it would be rude to just wander over on my own).

I never did visit when they had a bon fire, since that is when the boom happened. I was over my fear of the yard, but the fire triggered fear memories. My human decided it wasn't important to stress me by working on desensitizing me to the bon fire since they happened infrequently. I was happy to remain home during those times. The fear of my neighbor's yard was inhibiting my fun and ability to get attention from my neighbors, so that was a fear worth overcoming. Humans sometimes have to decide which fears are all right for a dog to have and which fears are unfounded and stifling. My human decided that a fear of fire was probably not a bad thing, so she didn't work on that aspect of my fears.

All the fears I've mentioned so far are ones connected with a negative experience. What people may not realize is lack of experience can also create fears. Many people get their dogs from shelters. This is definitely a noble choice, and one to be applauded. I've been at a shelter, and it's no fun. There are so many dogs who need a home and a second chance at life. Sometimes an adoption goes smoothly and all are happy with the choices made. Other times, it takes a while for a dog to settle into a new home.

People tend to fall in love with the poor little dog huddled in the back of a cage with nothing but fear in her big brown eyes. They want to save the dog from the cruel, cruel life she must have led to make her this way. All a dog needs is a loving home and all will be well, right? Well…not always. When a dog continues to show fears weeks later, the loving person is hurt.

"How can the dog be so ungrateful?" A loving person once exclaimed to my human as her dog huddled in a corner. "I gave her a home, love, food, water, and she still won't come to me. All dogs like me. She's just being stubborn."

The dog in this scenario wasn't being ungrateful or stubborn; the dog was just doing what worked for survival up to that point in her life. Until humans show the dog a new way of being, the dog will continue to react with fear. Just giving love is not enough. As a matter of fact, sometimes that love can actually increase the fear. If a person tells a dog, "It's all right" in a soothing voice while the dog is showing fear, they are in fact telling the dog it is all right to feel fear. The dog will need patience and guidance to learn to live a new way, and it usually takes time—lots of time. If you don't have the time, the patience, or the ability to accept a dog for who they are, then adopting a shy dog is probably not a good idea. There are steps you can take to help a shy dog gain confidence, but you must realize there's always a chance that the dog can only progress so far. Sometimes the shy nature is an underlying personality trait of the dog that can't totally be overcome. If you can't accept that, then a shy dog may not be a good fit for your family as a companion animal.

If your dog is showing shy issues with family members, then start out the same way my human did with me. She didn't say anything; she didn't ask anything of me; she didn't even look at me. We just sat. Fearful dogs need to have positive experiences. If you can't approach the dog, don't bother trying. Sit down in the middle of the room with a good book and a few pieces of kibble on the floor behind you and let the dog watch. If the dog comes over to investigate, ignore the dog completely. Don't look at the dog; don't talk to the dog; just let the dog approach and sniff. If the dog goes away after taking the kibble, put more kibble out. The idea is to teach the dog that you are not "up to something." This can take quite a while with some dogs. Others will learn a little quicker. It depends on the dog's personality and past experiences (or lack thereof) with people.

Dogs shouldn't be pushed to overcome fears. Sometimes that can cause a dog to become stressed, shut down, and then no learning will occur. Imagine being afraid of heights. Although people may tell you there is nothing to fear, you are still scared. Pushing you to the top of a high building and forcing you to look down over the edge is not necessarily going to help you overcome your fears. Most likely it will just make you angry at the person who pushed you to do it.

If I had been forced into the yard I feared, I may have developed more fears because I would have felt trapped. By gradually allowing me to learn on my own, I was able to be calm and retain the learning experience. Overcoming fears is about building trust. It's hard to trust someone who forces you into situations you are not ready to face.

If you are wondering what happened to Goldie, she learned that trash bins were not to be feared. Her human first played the "Find it" game at home with Goldie. She tossed treats on the ground and said "Find it." After playing this game at home without fear or any other distractions, Goldie and her human took it to the streets. They approached a trash bin and stopped before Goldie showed fear. Goldie's human had her do a few tasks, like a sit, down, and stay. They took a few more steps toward the trash bin and started to play the "Find it" game, again before Goldie showed fear. Slowly they worked their way up to the trash bin, tossing treats and keeping everything "jolly." Goldie eventually learned that there was nothing to fear about that particular trash bin. They repeated the steps down the road at each trash bin, until Goldie finally realized trash bins weren't anything to fear.

If your dog has a fear of other dogs, the "Find it" game can be helpful. Sniffing the ground while around other dogs is a calming signal and shows the other dogs that your dog means no harm. If a dog learns to sniff the ground instead of barking at other dogs, they soon find out that other dogs don't seem as threatening. (See the chapter on *Meeting and Greeting Other Dogs*.) If your dog is fearful of people, the steps to help a fearful dog learn to be around people are on the next page. Take the steps slowly. If the dog shows any signs of aggression, always seek professional help.

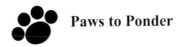 **Paws to Ponder**

Do not rush these steps. It could take weeks or months to progress through them. Not every dog will be able to overcome their fears 100%. However, if you ignore fear, it may intensify and turn into an aggression issue. Immediately begin to work on a fear when it first starts. Don't feel that it will pass with time. Usually fears increase when ignored. Take the time to help build your dog's confidence in as many situations as possible to help your dog live a long, happy, and well-adjusted life. Seek professional help if necessary to properly handle potential aggressive situations.

NOTE:

Teach loose leash walking before working on these steps. (See the Chapter entitled *These Paws Were Made for Walking* for instructions on teaching proper leash skills.)

Dealing with People Fears

1. Make sure the dog is really hungry so food is very appealing.

2. Put the dog on a 6' leash and keep the leash nice and loose. Do not pull or tighten on the leash at all. Your anxiety will transfer to the dog.

3. Give a friend some treats and have the friend walk AWAY from you with arms down at his sides and treats clearly visible to the dog in both hands.

4. Follow behind your friend and catch up to him. Allow the dog to sniff and take the food from the friend's hands. If the dog is hesitant to approach, have the friend drop the food and continue walking. Allow the dog to sniff and find the food while following behind your friend. Decrease the space between you and your friend gradually until the dog is comfortable taking food directly from his hand. At no time during this step should your friend make eye contact with the dog.

5. Have your friend put more food in his hands and repeat the whole process a few times.

6. Once this is going well, have your friend turn his body slightly toward the dog as the dog approaches from behind and takes the treat. Make sure there is still no eye contact.

More steps to go on the next page!

Fears Cont.

7. When the dog is finally comfortable with the friend turning his body, start having the dog approach with the person facing the dog. Have your friend stand still with hands at his sides, while you walk with the dog and approach the friend. At this point the dog knows the person has food and is usually willing to approach. If the dog is hesitant, have the person gently toss treats. If the dog still hesitates, the friend may need to squat down with his body turned slightly to the side and no eye contact to seem less threatening. Again, if aggression is involved, do not do this without professional help.

8. Repeat this approach a few times while the person is standing still. As that starts to go well, progress to having the person walking towards you as you walk towards them. Pretty soon your dog will be comfortable…with THIS friend.

9. Start all over with different individuals. Yup, you read it right. Start from the beginning. Your dog is used to only one person with the training done so far.

10. The goal is to get to a point where you can walk past people and your dog will relax. Your dog may never get to the point of loving other people, but if you can help your dog become more relaxed around people, it's a step in the right direction.

CAUTION:
Please seek professional help if your dog's fears include any growling, snapping, lunging, or biting. These are serious problems and should not be handled without proper professional guidance.

Chapter 19

Dogs and Cats Living Together in Harmony

Dogs and Cats Living Together in Harmony

Tales throughout the years have been told of the dislike that dogs have towards cats and vice versa. People often feel that the two cannot coexist, but that is not always the case. When introduced properly, cats and dogs can live in harmony.

I live with five cats, and we have all learned to coexist. I won't say that all the dogs love all the cats and vice versa, but we live together peacefully. Every time a new dog comes into the house, it's a process to go through the introductions again, but it's worth it.

My cat friends all have very different personality, so each one has to be taken into consideration before introducing any dog.

Dodger is rightly named because he dodges here and there and is a little on the nervous side. Dogs are more likely to chase Dodger, because he will run. Chase is a fun game most dogs will not ignore.

Izzy, on the other hand, will come right up to a dog and rub all over him. This can confuse dogs who are used to cats running. Some stand there baffled by Izzy's behavior, but others can be downright dangerous to her. Her trust in dogs turns her into an easy target.

Kaiser gets nervous on the inside. He freezes, stares at any new dog, and then proceeds to urinate around the house. He's not really great with changes in the household or in life in general. Kaiser is a target because he freezes and just stares. Staring is a threat to most dogs and can cause a dog to react negatively.

Princess, well, she doesn't really like any other animals, and she will bat with her paws at anyone who passes by. I learned to stay away from her, but visiting animals need to be shown how to handle the wrath of Princess. Again, her actions can get a dog riled up, or she can cause damage to a dog's face if her claws are out, which many times they are.

Sampson was a stray cat who roamed the neighborhood for a few years. He frequented our house for a while before he decided that our household was a friendly one...at least as far as the dogs and humans go. Sampson is not much of a cat lover, and he doesn't instantly trust dogs either. He hunches up his back, fluffs out, and hisses whenever an unfamiliar animal approaches, setting himself up for a nasty interaction.

How all these personalities mesh into one household is a topic for another book. This chapter is about how to help dogs get along with cats. I only mention the varying personalities of cats, because different personalities entice dogs in different ways. A herding dog may be more excited by a cat who runs. A bold dog may feel a cat who stares is more of a threat. There are some basic precautions and steps to take no matter what type of cat(s) share' your home.

Notice on these intro steps that the dog and cat are not loose together in the house. Once a chase ensues, it's harder to gain trust. Keeping everyone calm while in the same room is of upmost importance.

Intro

1. Set up a safe place for the cat to stay when you are not home. Make sure you have both a baby gate and a door to this area and that it is complete with a cat box and fresh water.

2. Have a crate for both the cat and dog. (See the chapter on *Crate Training* if the dog is not already crate trained.)

3. Put the dog in the crate and allow the cat to roam around and sniff the dog if desired. Distract the dog with some treats to prevent any barking or crazy behavior.

4. Now put the cat in a crate. Allow the dog to walk around the room and sniff the cat through the crate. Again, use treats to encourage calm behavior.

5. Feed both the cat and dog in crates side-by-side. Meals should only come when they are together so they learn good things happen when the other is around. If eating too close makes either one too nervous to eat, put some distance between the crates in the beginning and slowly move them closer together.

Don't stop here, there are mores steps to take!

Next...

5. Allow short supervised time together. If the dog has a high prey drive, keep the dog on a leash at all times while the cat is roaming loose. Do not hold the leash tightly, though, as this can increase aggression in some dogs.

6. It helps at this point if you have taught the "Leave It" cue from *The Basics* chapter. Some hissing and spitting is expected from cats, which may excite some dogs. Using the "Leave It" cue helps a dog learn to look away from the cat and ignore her.

7. Never leave a cat and dog alone in the house in the beginning. Even if they seem to be ignoring each other. Sometimes animals will ignore one another while they are checking the situation out. Don't get lulled into a false sense of security.

8. Once the cat and dog are getting along, you can leave them out together for short periods of time without being right there to supervise. Always keep a gate up in a room so the cat can escape from the dog if necessary. If you have an elderly cat, a small hole in a piece of wood in front of a doorway will help her get away from larger dogs. Little dogs are very difficult to escape from, but still annoying, so manage the situation to keep all safe until no one is showing fear of the other.

NOTE:

Always keep the cat food and litter boxes in an area inaccessible to the dog. It's important for cats to have a safe place to go. Plus cat food can pack on the pounds if a dog is eating it. The cats are not too happy about sharing either. Kitty crunchies (you know, the stuff the cats leave in the box) are incredibly tasty to dogs. It's best to keep all these temptations out of reach.

 Paws to Ponder

Take your time when introducing dogs and cats. The effort you make will be well worth it. I know it may seem like a lot of work, but once they have a bad experience with each other, it's much harder to get cats and dogs to develop a trusting relationship. Managing a difficult situation later is much harder than taking the right steps from the start. Whether you are introducing a new cat to a dog, or a new dog to a household cat, follow these steps, and don't rush them. Your animals will benefit and so will you.

Chapter **20**

Meeting and Greeting Other Dogs

Meeting and Greeting Other Dogs

Some dogs love to meet other dogs. They happily go to the dog park and instantly enjoy romping with old and new friends without hesitation. Then there are some dogs who just don't like other dogs at all. That's why it is so important not to let your dog rush up to another dog when walking until you ask the person if it is all right for the dogs to greet. Some dogs are a little more reserved and need time to check out the situation before rushing up to sniff another dog's rear end. Yes, sniff a rear. That's what dogs do. It's proper body language. I realize humans find this disgusting for whatever strange reason, but it's important that you let your dog do this very proper doggie greeting.

Imagine if a stranger came running up to you and gave you a hug. Most likely you would feel very uncomfortable with this up close and personal greeting. It's unconventional in the human world to greet a stranger with a hug. Perhaps some outgoing individuals may give a hug after a short introduction and chat, but never right up front when the two first greet. It's the same way in the dog world. We have rules on how to greet other dogs. Some dogs know these rules because they learned them from their mother, litter mates, or experiences with other dogs. Some dogs are clueless.

Lucas, a big black Lab, thought that everyone should love him. When he saw other dogs, he would gallop right up, and put his face in their face. Although the following dialog all occurred through body language, I put it in human terms for clarity so people can understand what occurs between nonverbal canines.

"Hi, there," Lucas said one day to a German Shepherd at the dog park getting right in his face while prancing around. "Let's play."

"Go away," the other dog snapped at Lucas. "You're rude. I don't even know you." He went back to sniffing the ground.

"What's there to know?" Lucas said as he pawed at the other dog's face and tried to get him to play. The other dog turned his back. Lucas walked around to his face.

"Let's play," he said with his paws as he jumped around and pawed at the other dog some more.

"Go awaaaay," the other dog growled.

"Play, play, play," Lucas ran circles around the dog and barked. The dog lunged and bit at Lucas. He ran and hid behind his human's legs in fear.

All Lucas wanted to do was play, and he might have been able to if he had greeted the German Shepherd properly first. Dogs have certain rituals to greeting. Easy-going, friendly dogs will usually approach each other and go straight to sniffing each other's rear. This gives all sorts of information about the other dog—like whether the dog is male or female, intact or not, scared or not (anal glands may express when a dog is scared). This information then helps the dog decide how to proceed. Some dogs will instantly go into a play bow (elbows on the ground, rear in the air, tail wagging) to let the other dog know they are ready to engage in some fun romping and running. If either dog has shown fear, then the dogs may sniff the grass in the area for a while waiting to see if things calm down. This may also be how dogs initially greet if they are leery of the situation. Many times people feel dogs don't like each other when they ignore the other dog and just sniff, but often we are just checking the situation out for a little while to assess what will happen next.

These are skills that Lucas did not possess. Almost every time he approached another dog, the dog would growl, snap, or bite at him. After a while, he decided that dogs were mean creatures to be guarded against. He began to growl, snap, and bite at other dogs who approached him.

If Lucas had been taught proper greeting manners in the beginning, his aggression towards other dogs may have been avoided. However, his human thought the way he met other dogs was cute because he was so dopey and friendly in her eyes. What she didn't realize was that Lucas broke every greeting rule in the dog world.

Turning a learned aggressive behavior around after the fact is much harder than teaching your dog to greet appropriately from the beginning. Lucas had to go through a lengthy training program to help him get over his fear of other dogs, which is what triggered the aggression.

On leash and NOT at the dog park, Lucas first had to learn a proper recall ("Come" cue) so his human would have more control over him. Some very friendly dogs helped by walking and training together with Lucas and his human. Every time Lucas started to approach a dog while both were on leash, he was called back by his human. *This helped him turn his back on other dogs and see that dogs don't growl when you do that.*

They took walks together at first with some distance between the dogs. The distance was decreased as Lucas began to relax. When they got close to the other dogs, his human threw treats on the ground, saying "Find it," a game they first played at home. Lucas knew those words meant treats were on the ground, and he stopped to look for them. *This helped him see that other dogs don't bark and growl if you sniff the ground first.*

Lucas started to walk behind another dog, and then approached and sniffed the other dog's rear end. *This taught Lucas the appropriate way to greet instead of instant face contact.*

Lucas learned new ways to interact with dogs. As he began to greet and play properly, Lucas discovered dogs don't always growl and snap. Lucas became less defensive and happy to see other dogs.

Some dogs need guidance from people on the most basic doggie skills. When a dog is taken away from a litter too early (eight weeks should be the earliest, but 10 – 12 weeks is even better), they don't get a chance to learn from their litter mates about proper greetings. Other dogs who were with their litter mates for a while, may not have learned all their lessons or they may have forgotten over the years. Perhaps they were the bullies of the litter, picking on everyone else and none of the pups corrected them for it. Some dogs who have been kenneled part of their life with no dog interaction, just don't know what to do with other dogs when they finally get a chance to meet one. Whatever the reason, humans need to watch their dogs and redirect any inappropriate greeting or playing techniques. If dogs don't seem to understand the rules, take the time to teach them before problems develop.

Paws to Ponder

The steps Lucas went through took a long time and had a professional trainer involved making sure all participants were safe. If the steps had been taken prior to Lucas developing a fear of other dogs, he would have learned proper greeting methods faster and would have avoided developing a fear of other dogs. Watch your dog, learn what skills they do and don't have, and take time to redirect your dog's behavior to more appropriate reactions. If you are unsure how to do that or are worried about you or your dog's safety, seek professional help. Dog aggression is a serious problem and can often lead to your dog biting another dog and also hurting a person. People often reach in to save their dog when an attack happens and inadvertently get bitten. Some dogs are fine off-leash but become aggressive towards other dogs on leash. Take the time to train your dog to relax around other dogs on and off a leash. It could be a matter of life or death.

Chapter 21

Dog Parks
and
Your Dog

Dog Parks and Your Dog

Playing with other dogs can be really fun and great exercise, but you should consider a few points about your dog before taking him to a dog park. First and foremost, does your dog come when called at home? If not, you should teach this skill first before ever stepping into a dog park. (See *The Basics* chapter for further instructions on teaching this important cue.) You need to be able to have control over your dog at the park at all times.

Second, aggressive dogs should never be brought to the dog park. This is not a situation to teach your dog to be nice to others. Professional help should be sought before attempting to bring a dog with aggression tendencies to a dog park (if ever).

Third, if your dog is shy around other dogs, a dog park may not be the right place to have your dog play. Set up smaller groups of friendly dogs to socialize shy dogs in order to create a more positive experience. If you don't know any dogs to set up small groups with, go to the park on a day that is less busy. Dog parks can help shy dogs overcome their fears, but if there are too many dogs descending all at once, it may also enhance and confirm fears.

Finally, puppies under four months (sometimes even six months) should not go to the dog park to keep them safe and make sure they do not learn inappropriate behaviors. Socialization for young pups should be controlled by taking a puppy class and walking the dog on leash around town ensuring that all greetings are a positive experience. Playing too rough at a young age can cause a puppy physical harm by putting too much pressure on joints. Controlled play for short periods is much safer for young dogs.

Having said all that, dog parks can be great fun! I love nothing better than seeing my friends at the park and having a good romp or game of ball. The following are suggested steps to make sure the dog park experience is positive for both you and your dog.

Just Getting In the Dog Park

FYI:

Going to the dog park is a privilege. I have to earn the right to go in the park. That means walking nicely, entering politely, and sitting to have my leash taken off. If I don't do any of those things, it's back to the car. I know my human means it too; she's done it before when I tested her, so I make sure I follow the rules so I can play with my friends. It's hard to be good when you are excited, but learning calm behavior is a good thing.

1. Keep your dog on a leash as you approach the dog park. There are cars and people around, and it is safer to have your dog on a leash. Plus a leash will help keep your dog calm as you approach the dog park.

2. Walk your dog up to the dog park with a loose leash. Do not allow your dog to pull ahead. The dog needs to know that you are in control up to and in the dog park. (See *These Paws Were Made for Walking* for loose leash walking instructions.)

3. I like to have a little time to sit outside of the dog park before entering the fenced area. (Never take your dog to a park without a secure fence.) Sitting outside the fence allows me and my human to size up the situation. If the play looks too uncontrolled, my human may decide not to enter. I don't like dogs who come straight up in my face, so if there are a lot of dogs who do that, we may decide to come to the park another day. Sometimes watching just gives us time to decide which dogs we may want to avoid.

4. Once inside the park, I have to sit while my human takes off my leash. If I get too excited and forget to sit, my human will take me back out of the park. I learned quickly to sit right away when I enter the park. It's important to take your dog's leash off, as she may feel threatened when other dogs approach if you leave the leash on.

At the Park

NOTE:

Constantly interact with your dog while at the park. This is your dog's time, not social time for you. Learning to listen with all the distractions of a dog park will make your dog very well-behaved. Plus it will impress all your friends.

If a situation arises at the dog park that makes you uncomfortable, trust your instincts, get your dog, and leave.

1. When the leash is removed, my human gives me permission to "Go play." She walks with me and watches me the whole time. Occasionally she calls me to her, and then allows me to go play again. If I don't listen and come when called, I know she will come get me and make me leave the park, so I have learned to listen. Don't keep calling to your dog if your dog ignores you. If your dog does not come, go get him.

2. Sometimes we play games at the park. I do some of my tricks while other dogs are around so I learn to listen better. My reward is going to play with my friends again. If there aren't many dogs at the park, my human and I will play ball.

3. When it's time to leave the park, my human comes over to me and asks me to walk with her to the gate. She then asks me to sit and hooks the leash on my collar. This one took a while for me to learn, but I now know that we will get to go to the park again. Plus she always has a yummy cookie waiting for me when we get back to the car.

4. Don't bring treats into the dog park, you might get mugged by a bunch of dogs. Plus some dogs don't like to share food. It's better to keep all food rewards in the car. Playing is the reward to use in the park.

Paws to Ponder

Your dog may be nervous the first time at a dog park. It's best to start out during quieter times at the park. Weekday afternoons are usually a little less busy than weekends. Watch your dog for signs of stress—cowering, head lowering, lip licking, yawning, ears back, trying to avoid another dog. If you don't like how a dog is playing with your dog, call your dog away and go to another part of the park or leave. Dogs may pick up bad habits from other dogs, so choose your dog's friends wisely.

Chapter **22**

The Blessed Addition:

Bringing Home Baby

The Blessed Addition—Bringing Home Baby

People love their dogs—perhaps too much at times. I know it sounds strange to say that people can overly love their dogs, but it's a common problem that can create serious behavior issues. Actually, it's not the love, but what people consider love, that causes the problem.

A dog is often the first "child" in a family. A young couple gets a puppy and raises the dog as a surrogate baby. They give the dog unlimited toys and access to all furniture. In essence, they spoil the dog rotten. Soon the dog believes that she is the ruler of the household.

Then one day, the couple decides to have a human baby. Many times, the dog is not given a second thought while preparing for the arrival of this blessed addition. When the day finally comes to bring baby home, they present the baby to the dog, who may sniff and lick at the baby. That's when it all begins. Grandma freaks out about dog germs, and the dog is escorted out of the room. The dog sits in the backyard wondering what in the world just happened, and associates these new undesirable human behaviors with the baby.

Day-after-day similar events happen. The baby takes all of his human's attention away. The dog becomes confused and frustrated with the changes. When the baby is put down for a nap, finally the dog receives some much needed playtime and love from the humans. The dog makes the connection that the baby being in the room is bad, and the baby being gone is good. This is NOT what you want your dog to believe. Frustration in a dog may lead to aggressive outbursts.

Luckily, this frustration can be avoided with careful planning and preparation prior to bringing your baby home. I happen to love children. They are sweet and innocent and always willing to give a good belly rub. However, not all dogs see it that way. You may be blessed with a dog who accepts a baby without question, but don't wait to find out if this is the case when the baby is born. Taking steps ahead of time to prepare your dog for a new family member is a good idea.

Before even thinking about doing any training involving children with your dog, consider your dog's temperament. This is a time for honesty not excuses. If you are unsure how your dog behaves, find a professional trainer who is versed in dog body language to help you.

If you answer "yes" to any of the following questions, it's time for some professional help.

1. Does your dog lash out at strangers? Lashing out includes lunging, barking, air snapping, nipping, biting.

2. Is your dog protective of food, you, or toys? Dogs should be able to have anyone come up and take food or toys away. Anyone should be able to come up to you and pet your dog (with permission of course).

Dogs need to be reliable around children and if you cannot honestly answer "yes" to the above questions, please seek professional help before children come to your home. Planning to keep the dog locked up when children visit, only increases the dog's dislike of visitors. This problem should not be ignored. If a baby is due to live in your house, managing the situation by locking the dog up is just not feasible most of the time. Someone is bound to leave a door open and endanger the child.

O.K. so I've nagged you enough about all that. I feel very strongly about this training. Many of my dog friends have been sent to shelters or worse, because they weren't reliable around children. I take this baby/children training stuff seriously. Whether your dog is big like me or little, this training is very important.

The following steps offer some ideas to help your dog accept a baby into what he considers HIS home. If the baby is already in the home, skip to the steps entitled *Day-to-day With Baby and Dog* and implement immediately.

Grandparents: If you have grandchildren who visit, even occasionally, you should initiate the steps to make sure your dog is safe around children.

1.   Dogs need training no matter what is about to happen in the home, but it's even more important when bringing a baby into the household. Your dog should learn at least the basics of sit, down, come, and stay. (See the chapter entitled *The Basics*.) These cues will come in handy when you need to focus your attention on the baby. It will allow the dog to be present in the same room as you and your baby and give you control of the situation.

2. Establish rules prior to the baby coming home. If certain areas of the house will become off-limits when the baby arrives, start teaching this immediately. The idea is that you don't want any new restrictions to be associated with the baby coming into the house, or your beloved animal companion may become frustrated with the changes and act out in unpleasant ways. It's best to make all changes long before the new baby comes home.

3. Invite a friend over with their children so that your dog will have the opportunity to experience little people. Children move quickly, squeal loudly, and pet roughly. Your dog needs to get used to the sights, sounds, and smells of children. Watch very closely for any negative reactions. To be fair to the dog, redirect children who are too rough. If your dog is trying to get away from interactions, allow the dog to do so.
Only do this if your dog is usually friendly.

**Prep Cont:
Role Playing**

Note: Preparing your dog prior to the baby coming home will make the transition easier for all involved. Don't assume your dog will love the new addition. Do some training in advance to head off any potential problems.

This one may seem a little silly, but do it anyway. Think of it as tapping into your inner-child. Dogs like it when humans find their inner-child because they are usually so much more fun!

Role-play with your dog. (You read that right.) Go through the actions of what you will be doing with the baby, so your dog will become accustomed to your new ways.

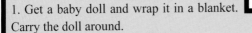

1. Get a baby doll and wrap it in a blanket. Carry the doll around.

2. Take it to the changing table and put your dog in a sit-stay while you change the baby doll.

3. Put the doll on the floor on a blanket with baby toys around and put your dog in a down stay.

4. Create a section of the room just for the dog. Make this area off-limits to the baby, so your dog will have a place to go away from ear-pulling when the baby begins to crawl. Establish this place from the beginning. Add a crate with a soft bed for your dog's comfort and safety. It can also be used as a place to send the dog to chew on a toy when you need time to be with the baby. The dog will associate this place with good things, not a time-out from family fun if you make it a great place before the baby even comes home.

Note: Teaching your dog to sit to greet prior to bringing the baby home will make homecoming much more controlled. Your dog will be excited to see you, but if he already knows proper greeting skills, you will be able to introduce him to the baby much quicker than a dog with no previous training.

Bringing Baby Home

1. Have someone bring home a blanket that the baby was wrapped in so that the dog can get used to this new scent before the baby comes home.

2. You may have been gone a few days, and the dog missed you. If you ignore the dog when you come in, the dog will be frustrated and confused. Have a neutral person (grandma or a neighbor) actually carry the new baby into the house to leave Mom and Dad free to greet the dog once the dog calms down.

3. Once the homecoming excitement dies down, let your dog get acquainted with the baby. Sit in a comfortable chair and let your dog sniff the baby. Most people don't want their animals to lick the baby, but this is their way of getting to know someone. The baby will come in contact with more germs from well-wishers than from your dog as long as you keep your dog healthy with regular veterinarian visits and deworming. Redirect any overenthusiastic licking, but one or two little slurps will usually do no harm. If this totally grosses you out or your dog just gets too excited when licking, redirect the dog away from licking with a toy or treats.

The Most Important Step on the Next Page!

Day-to-Day with Dog and Baby

DON'T SKIP THESE STEPS...PLEASE! These will help ensure the safety of your baby and the ability to have your dog always be part of the family's activities. Many of my dog friends end up thrown into a backyard or chained to a tree because people don't feel comfortable with their dog around the baby. Following these steps will help everyone learn to get along.

1. This one is important. It's opposite from what most people do: Be sure to establish some play times with your dog when the baby is PRESENT—not just when the baby is napping in another room. People often make the mistake of paying attention to the dog only when the baby is gone. The dog then associates the baby being gone as a good thing. If Mom and Dad reverse this by being fun only when the baby is around and ignore the dog when the baby is out of the room, then your dog will want the baby in the room. Soon the baby and dog will be best buds, because the baby is the key to all good things happening. If the dog is locked up every time the baby is out and playing, the dog may become frustrated. If you must put your dog in a crate, be sure to give a special toy and keep the crate close by.

2. Always, always provide constant supervision with dogs and children no matter how much you trust your dog. Accidents can always happen even with the most trustworthy animals. I'm a one-hundred-dred pound St. Bernard, and although I'm extremely gentle with children, I have big paws and don't always think about where I am putting them. If I get excited, I just react. Even big, gentle, well-trained dogs like me shouldn't be left alone with children in a room. Don't get lulled into a false sense of security. Dogs are animals, and we don't usually think about the results of our actions.

166

Children and dogs can be great together. I like babies because they make humans silly when they talk! I like toddlers because I can walk along and help them learn to walk. Older children are great because they throw balls. Dogs will learn to adapt to a new member of the family as long as you take time to introduce us to this new member and the new rules that go along with the addition.

Take time to make sure this union goes smoothly, especially if your dog has been an established member of your family for some time prior to a baby being introduced. Children and dogs are always learning. Teach both of them what your expectations are each step of the way.

Child Training

Your dog isn't the only one who needs training. Children should be taught too. Don't expect your dog to put up with abuse from a child. Show your child how to be gentle with your dog. Some dogs don't mind being crawled all over, but everyone has their limits. Be fair to your dog and watch your child closely. We don't want to bite if we don't have to, but sometimes when our growls or attempts to get away are ignored, we are left with no choice.

Teaching children to be kind and gentle to animals is the first step to keeping your child safe around dogs. Also teaching your child what to do around strange dogs is a good idea. Teach your child that whenever a dog approaches to greet the best way to behave is to stand still and allow the dog to sniff. Running around excites dogs. Practice standing like a tree or curling up like a rock if the child should fall on the ground. Also teach your child to ask to pet an animal before reaching out. It may be cute that your child hugs your dog, but not all dogs like that. If your child doesn't learn this, he may one day go up to hug a dog who doesn't appreciate hugs and get bitten in the face. An ounce of prevention around dogs is always the way to ensure the safety of your child and your dog.

Paws to Ponder

Plan ahead, and train your dog prior to the baby coming home. Make sure all animals in the house are up-to-date on vaccinations and deworming. Ignore the dog when the baby is asleep and play with the dog when the baby is around, never leave the dog alone with the baby—not for a second. That's all it takes for an accident to happen even with the nicest dog. Better yet, those of you reading this who are planning to get a dog but haven't yet, when you do get the dog start setting rules from the very beginning. Don't "love" the dog with lots of stuff and no limits. A healthy, well-adjusted dog is one who has rules and just a few toys. If you can't resist buying new toys, rotate the toys every few weeks. Then your dog will feel like he has something new and be entertained while you are busy with the baby.

Chapter 23

I'm Bored

I'm Bored

It was a lovely sunny afternoon, and I was in the backyard enjoying some fresh air. I watched mesmerized as my human hung clothes on a line that spun around in a circle. Hypnotized by the clothes that dangled and fluttered in the breeze, I didn't even notice when my human went inside. Suspended on a pole, the line swung around and around as a gentle breeze blew across the yard. The whirligig beckoned to me. I could resist no longer, I jumped up and grabbed a piece of clothing and tugged to my heart's content. When it released itself from the clip that held it tightly to the line, I dropped it and proceeded to the next item of clothing. What fun! I pulled; I shook; I dragged the clothes around the yard. Soon all the clothes were pulled from the line, and I tired of the game. Contented and exhausted from my activities, I went over to a shady spot in the yard and settled for a nice little nap. A harsh screech startled me from my slumber.

"What happened here?" The woman of the house screeched at the top of her lungs as she came out into the yard and looked around. "Delilah, I know you did this. Where are you?"

I could tell by her tone of voice that she was not happy. I slunk out from my cozy spot, and sidled up to her with my cutest "Aren't I adorable" look. It didn't help.

"You stupid dog. What were you thinking? I put you out here to enjoy a nice day and look what you did. Dumb dog. You are more trouble than you are worth." She ranted on, but I didn't understand the words, only her tone of voice. When she was finished, she picked up the clothes and stomped into the house.

"You stay here. I don't want to look at you." She slammed the door and left me outside.

I had no idea what was wrong. I sighed, turn around, and slowly walked back to my cozy spot. People can be so mysterious. She put me outside to entertain myself and when I did, she got angry. I just don't get the human species sometimes.

When dogs are left to their own devices, without anything to do, they get bored. Bored dogs find entertainment. If you do not provide enough stimulation for dogs, they will find their own. What they choose to do may not be fitting with what humans would prefer them to do.

Dogs aren't alone in their boredom. I've heard human children say, "I'm bored. There's nothing to do," more than once during summer vacation. If left to their own devices, human children also find inappropriate ways to deal with their boredom. It's no different for dogs. We need to be challenged. We need stimulation. There are also plenty of times that we need supervision.

A walk every day, a couple of times a day, helps a dog get out and explore. Off-leash running and playing in a safe location allows a dog time to exercise and investigate. Train your dog to learn new challenges. Oliver, my Poodle friend, learned to play the piano. He has a blast banging away and singing. Sometimes I sing along with him. It may sound like noise to the human ear, but it is pure joy for us. It's something our human taught Oliver to help stimulate his mind and keep him busy, which in turn keeps him out of trouble. When he doesn't get exercise for both his mind and body, he can be rather troublesome indeed.

I used to run away from my home when I was left alone. I missed people and would escape from the yard to seek interaction and entertainment with others. My houdini and wandering ways are some of the reasons I got into trouble and had to move from home-to-home so much. A bored dog will seek out entertainment even if it isn't a safe alternative. I didn't understand about streets and cars, I was just looking for some fun.

If you work all day, hire a dog sitter to come in mid-day to play with and walk your dog. Dog sitters are great fun and help break up a long boring day of being home alone. Take time to hide treats and toys around the house and teach the dog to go treasure hunting. This is a fun game while humans are gone. You have to show us how the game works by starting to hide things and showing us where they are, but our noses usually catch on to the game quickly. Then put some kind of cue to it like "Go hunt" or "Find treasures," using the cue as you leave the house. Instead of the dog being anxious over you leaving, she will show excitement at the prospect of a fun hunt.

Dogs should be part of the family. I never understood why people got a dog and then left him outside alone. Where's the companionship in that? My friend Jasper, a German Shepherd, was kenneled the first year of his life. He didn't have enough interaction with people and other animals. When he was adopted, he had to learn all about the world and social graces with both people and dogs. Please don't leave a dog outside all the time. A dog kept out in the yard all day will definitely get bored, and possibly do a lot of damage, learn how to escape, or bark excessively and disturb the neighbors. Walk, socialize, train, and play with us. Otherwise you may end up with a bored dog who picks her own entertainment. Those swinging clothes sure were fun! (See the chapter entitled *Helping the Chew-a-holic* for more ideas on toys to help entertain dogs.)

Paws to Ponder

Some breeds require more time and attention than others. Working breeds require extensive exercise, training, and interactive time with you to avoid boredom. If you do not have time to commit to these high energy dogs, consider another breed. Do your homework and learn what breed is best for your family lifestyle even if you are looking at shelters with mixed breeds. Take your best guess about the breed type and then make an educated decision about your choice.

Conclusion

Closing Words from Delilah and Cheryl

By no means has this book covered all the issues people may encounter with their dogs. Dogs and humans have lived together for thousands of years, which is plenty of time to develop a ton of problems. As dogs grow in popularity as companions in our communities, more and more laws are passed governing our dogs' behavior. Now more than ever, it is important to train your dog to be a good canine citizen.

Over the years there have been a lot of changes to how we teach dogs. Those changes will continue to occur. A plethora of books appear on shelves with a number of methods . The humane steps taught in this book have proved to work well if applied correctly and consistently with love and patience. There are more in-depth instructions in other books. We tried to keep the steps basic and fun to ease the training process. Please see the *Suggested Reading* list if you would like to learn more and develop better precision while training your dog.

Don't wait until problems occur. Establish rules, communicate those rules through positive methods, and take the time to understand a behavior problem from the dog's perspective.

Sometimes management is the best solution to a problem. If your dog gets into the garbage, perhaps it's just easier to lock the garbage in a cabinet. After all, it's mighty tempting stuff. If your dog gets on the furniture when you are gone, leave the cushions crooked, or use a mat with little points on it to make the couch uncomfortable (plastic rug runners turned upside-down often work well). If your dog gets food on the counter, don't leave food out. It's all common sense if you think about it. Dogs will be dogs. If a behavior is rewarding, it will be repeated—plain and simple. Eliminate the reward for undesired behaviors, and eventually you eliminate the inappropriate behavior. Understanding this concept will make your life with a dog so much easier. Yes, dogs need to learn rules, but humans also need to learn what is reasonable to expect from dogs.

As this journey of the world *In Delilah's Eyes* comes to a close, we wish you well as you go forth and enhance the bond with your canine companion with new understanding, appreciation, and unconditional love.

Train, enjoy, and love that wonderful, glorious creature we call Dog.

> Delilah and Cheryl—
> Bound together forever
> in furry slobbery love.

Suggested Reading

In Delilah's Eyes only scratched the surface of training and communicating with your canine companion. Our goal was to provide a quick simple yet fun guide to start you on a positive training path. For those who may want a more in-depth look at training techniques and an enhanced education on how to better communicate and understand your dog, the following are great books to do just that.

Getting Started: Clicker Training for Dogs--Karen Pryor
Getting in TTouch with Your Dog--Linda Tellington-Jones
The Power of Positive Thinking--Pat Miller

Coming June 2010 by Cheryl Falkenburry

Oliver's Occupation:
Jobs to Help Dogs Go from Zany to Zen
A Book of Tips and Tricks

Index